THE SMILE
OF A
DOLPHIN

THE SMILE OF A DOLPHIN

Remarkable Accounts of Animal Emotions

EDITED BY MARC BEKOFF

DISCOVERY BOOKS

NEW YORK

CONTENTS

chapter one
LOVE

PAGES PRECEDING TITLE PAGE:
Greetings between timber wolves, who are extremely loyal to their eight- to fifteen-member packs. Packs have rigid hierarchies reinforced by ritual body language, muzzle nips, and fights.

LEFT: *A female orangutan nurtures her infant. In the Malay language, orang means "man" and utan is derived from* hutan, *which means "forest."*

chapter two
FEAR, AGGRESSION, AND ANGER

chapter three
JOY AND GRIEF

chapter four
FELLOW FEELINGS

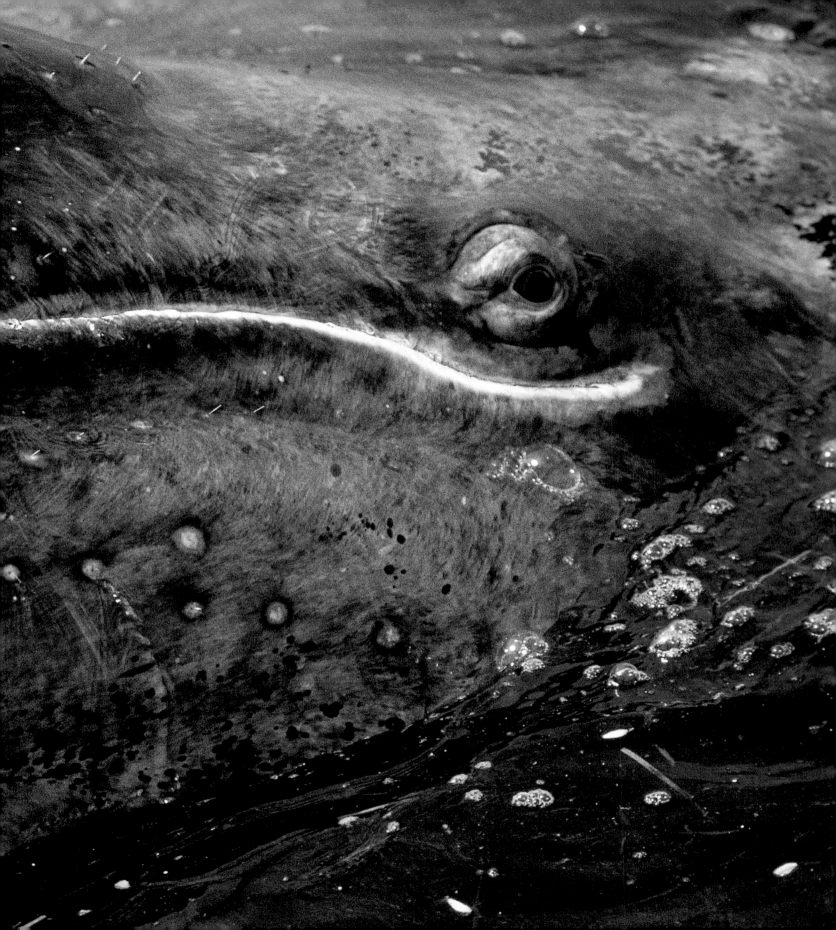

A Lover's Quarrel

Stephen Jay Gould

PRECEDING PAGES:

Gray whales like this three-week-old calf in the Baja Peninsula's Magdalena Bay surface for their first breath within ten seconds of their birth. Within thirty minutes they learn to swim.

LEFT: *Male great egrets battle for territory. Fighting often begins in the trees or on the ground and continues in the air until one of the birds is eventually driven off.*

Contrary to popular belief and stereotype, people who study animals in a scientific way do not generally treat them as unconscious mechanical automata and do not restrict their interest to objective and measurable properties (heart rates for physiology, for instance, or times for running through mazes) that can be experimentally determined and then replicated in well-controlled, simplified, and artificial systems of laboratory cages. Most biologists and psychologists entered this field of study because they love animals and find the diversity and richness of their behaviors—including the major differences and eerie likenesses when compared with the common actions of human beings—so primally fascinating and also so theoretically engaging.

Nonetheless, the norms of scientific study and prose do impose preferences for two styles of work and writing that tend to push to a periphery, or to eliminate entirely from consideration, the admittedly ambiguous (and sometimes nebulous) observations that best display the subtle complexity and individuality of animal behavior, and that also document the common bonds between their modes of cognition and ours. First, science does properly stress those clearly repeatable observations that can be manipulated and confidently evoked under experimental protocols—rather than the unique or rare behaviors that animals can display at odd moments in the complexities of their natural lives and ecologies (the so-called "anecdotes" of our deprecations). Second, scientific writing favors (and editors of professional journals often demand) the utterly depersonalized style of passive-voice description: "It was observed that, when suckling their neonates, the heart rates of these pigs became elevated to an extent...." This approach is virtually guaranteed to make a literary (and, I would say, biological) mockery of observations that would lose neither rigor nor accuracy if they were described in the ordinary language of empathy and activity.

These conventions, however understandable in origin and function, place unfair and impossible barriers before evolutionary biologists who wish to confer scientific legitimacy upon our major source of potential information about the emotional richness of animal lives, or at least of those animals sufficiently close to us in genealogy that we can claim at least some visceral understanding of the mental states behind facial expressions and bodily reactions sufficiently similar to our own to evoke a suspicion of true commonality by evolutionary continuity. (By contrast, I cannot imagine what causes an amoeba to move away from waters that we would regard as unpleasantly hot—and I would never use such terms as "pain" or direct "adaptation to avoid danger" in trying to understand such an interesting phenomenon.)

This unfairly banished source—called "anecdote" or "subjective story" in the usual dismissive mode—must be revalued and reinstated into science under its old and honored descriptor: the case study. Careful descriptions of complex and unique occurrences—salient actions done once by one organism in one unusual circumstance—form the pith and moment of all historical study, the source of history's crucial episodes, and the best entrée for understanding the full range and capability of any subject (and not a set of meaningless, discardable, and hopelessly subjective frills). History happens because Alexander died young, St. Paul had the gift of gab and organization, and Heisenberg miscalculated the amount of uranium needed to build a bomb—and not only because nature operates under spatiotemporally invariant laws of simple mathematical form. (Oliver Sacks has labored—much abetted by his brilliant literary style—to foment a similar fundamental change in the science of medicine: to bring back the careful and compassionate "case study," the story of an individual's unique mental and bodily life, to the center of scientific understanding of human health.)

The authors of this book pursue a similar lover's quarrel with scientific convention. They write these case studies from their own experiences—not the luck of casual and fortuitous moments, but the distillation of a best and most revealing particular from a lifetime of expertise under Pasteur's dictum that "fortune favors the prepared mind." In short, they write as scientists who know that unusual moments build the gateways to genuine historical understanding, and not as philistine or romantic worshipers of the sacred ineffable soul of organic naturalness, so often perverted by the cold emptiness of scientific armies. (In fact, this assumed cold emptiness is another ridiculous stereotype that must be abandoned as we recognize the potential for a unified and reinforcing science of animal behavior now within our reach if we can forge the data of careful case studies of unique behaviors with information gained by conventional methods of experimental validation for general rules of ordinary actions.)

Finally, while the scientific experts of this volume present their case studies to pursue their lover's quarrel with conventional limitations upon our understanding of the rich (and highly functional) emotional lives of animals, I must mention my own lover's quarrel with many of the stories in this book—a sure sign of a volume's vibrancy when the writer of a preface must engage the authors in his own dialogue of doubt amidst his prevailing pleasure. Bravo for case stud-

ies, and bravo for the inevitable "subjectivity" within any product of this genre. But all the more reason—given the dubiety, even the hostility, of many colleagues—for taking special care to avoid the genuine and serious pitfalls that led the doubters to their exaggerated reactions of pure dismissal in the first place. Yes, we are human and cannot avoid the language and knowledge of our own emotional experience when we describe a strikingly similar reaction observed in another species. But anthropomorphism remains a genuine barrier to understanding these different worlds, and I really doubt that Kierkegaard's issues can bear any more than the most distantly metaphorical (and almost surely misleading) relation to a whale's concerns.

Secondly, and to mention a longstanding personal complaint, I do wish that Darwinian observers of mentalities so different from our own would stretch the horizons of their potential explanations beyond the *summum bonum* of struggle for reproductive advantage in natural selection. I do accept the primacy of this Darwinian motor, but the rich and eerily different world of organic complexity—the very intricacy that leads these superb naturalists to reject the artificial confines of the laboratory as a sole source of knowledge and to embrace the case study in complex nature as a coequal realm for understanding—contains so many more things, motives, reasons, and oddities than we have ever dreamed of in Darwin's or anyone else's restricted human philosophy. Few phrases can trump the liberating power of "I don't know." If we can learn how to listen in the voices of undreamt possibilities (rather than only in the tones of familiar and comforting theories), we might distill some stunning surprises from those "endless creatures most beautiful and most wonderful" that Darwin chose to highlight in the closing sentence of *The Origin of Species*.

Japanese macaques, or snow monkeys, huddle in winter near a hot spring in a mountainous region northwest of Tokyo. Huddling behavior depends on species—some animals prefer to curl up alone.

ABOVE: *Male and female Laysan albatrosses, like these on Midway Atoll in the Hawaiian Islands, share incubation duties.*
RIGHT: *A male lion in Kenya watches as a cub explores.*

MIXING SCIENCE AND EMOTION

Marc Bekoff

Anyone who's spent much time with animals needs no convincing that we humans are not the only creatures on earth with rich emotional lives. To experience the caperings of a ferret or receive the caresses of a cat, to observe the grief of an orphaned chimpanzee or watch the bounding joy of a puppy at play, is to know—with an instinctive, intuitive certainty—that our animal kin have feelings. But the certainty of the lay person is not necessarily the certainty of the scientist.

A male silverback mountain gorilla needs a good threat display like this in order to found and lead his own social group of five to thirty others of both sexes.

Science requires more than intuition and instinct. It demands theories, experiments, data collection, outcome assessments, replication of results. Science can't merely know; it has to prove. And proving what animals feel—or even that they feel—can be infinitely frustrating. Even the word "emotion" is hard to define. Most of us believe we understand what we mean by it (it has to do with feelings—with love, hate, fear, joy, happiness, grief, despair, empathy, jealousy, anger, relief, disgust), but nevertheless the term isn't easily corralled into useful scientific parameters. For our purposes, let's say that emotions are psychoneural processes that express themselves as mood. But where does that leave us? Emotions still defy science's empirical method. They're subjective, fleeting, evanescent, elusive, and subject to the bias of the observer. We may know with some accuracy what we ourselves feel and how we express those feelings, and from there we go on to deduce the feelings of other people from how they look and behave. More often than not, our deductions are probably right. But can we truly, verifiably, know the feelings of another human being, much less those of a member of a different species?

For centuries, science's prevailing attitude toward the question of nonhuman emotion might be summed up as, "No, animals don't feel, or if they do we can't prove it, and in any case it doesn't much matter, since they're only animals." This line of thought followed the lead of seventeenth-century French philosopher René Descartes, who helped sire the scientific method with his get-down-to-basics dictum: "I think, therefore I am." Animals, declared Descartes, are merely automata, responding mechanically to whatever stimuli confront them. Feelings are no part of the equation. (Humans are different, he said, because of the "ghost in the machine"—a divine inspiration that informs our nature, and ours alone.)

Descartes's intellectual heirs over the years have been many. Most notable among them in the twentieth century was Harvard-based psychologist B. F. Skinner, who, with his doctrine of behaviorism, pushed Descartes's mechanistic theory to a new level: For all animals, including humans, behavior consists of responses to stimuli— no less, no more. Fear is simply a set of bodily reactions to a frightening stimulus, love a constellation of reactions to something attractive, and so forth. The effect of mechanistic philosophy was largely to dismiss animals and to deem them unworthy of legitimate scientific study—except, of course, when they proved useful in inquiries that were aimed at benefiting human beings.

A young red-necked wallaby in Australia's Queensland outback begs for its mother's attention.

But the prevailing historical view bracketed by Descartes and Skinner has not been the only one, nor even the one with the most credible adherents. No lesser a light than Charles Darwin, one of the most revolutionary and influential thinkers of any age, was among the first scientists to give serious attention to the question of animal emotions. Darwin's theory of evolution, proposed in the mid–nineteenth century and now accepted in some form by almost all scientists, argued for an

unfolding continuum of life on earth, one that implies a mental, physical, and emotional connection among humans and many other creatures. In fact, said the great naturalist, "the lower animals, like man, manifestly feel pleasure and pain, happiness, and misery." He believed that differences in emotions among us and our animal kin, and among a variety of nonhuman species, are a matter of degree, not kind.

As physical sciences such as genetics and neurobiology made exponential progress in the twentieth century, they tended to confirm Darwin's conclusions. Neurobiologists found, for instance, that certain structures in the human brain that are believed to govern emotions have analogous structures in the brains of certain other vertebrates. Moreover, the human and nonhuman brains share neurochemicals bearing on emotion that aren't merely analogous but are exactly the same. Isn't it logical to assume, then, that the neurological apparatus that give rise to our own feelings produce the same or similar emotions in them?

A correlative truth seems to be embedded in DNA, the fundamental blueprint for life. Researchers have found that we and our closest primate kin, the chimpanzees, share 98.4 percent of our genetic material. We share 97.7 percent with gorillas, 96.4 percent with orangutans. Surely it's the height of illogic (not to say arrogance) to assume that somehow, in the few strands of nucleic acids that separate us from our closest cousins on the evolutionary tree, emotions that are wholly absent in them suddenly blossomed in us.

Things have changed. Today, great numbers of scientists (and I certainly number myself among them) accept that nonhuman animals do experience emotions, and it's the naysayers who are on the defensive, clinging to creeds widely regarded as threadbare and outworn.

Still, the skeptical voices urge caution, and their objections must be addressed. They warn, for instance, against the pitfall of anthropomorphism, the attributing of human traits to nonhuman animals. And they have a point. It's both presumptuous and dangerous to blindly assume that animal emotions are exactly the same as ours, inspired by the same stimuli and with the same ramifications. A wolf cub romping with its littermates may not feel precisely the same pleasure as that of a human child frolicking with his playmates. And it's true that animals are best studied in their own environment and understood on their own terms. But where are we to start if not with ourselves? Surely it's rational, even necessary, to extrapolate in order to understand other creatures, and to use our own abilities and language to better comprehend theirs. We don't emit clicking sounds as dolphins do because we are not dolphins. Does that mean, however, that we should make no effort to understand dolphins and accept what they have to teach us? I think not. Even so, say the skeptics, anthropomorphism is surely a hazard when studying creatures very different from ourselves or when describing the subtler emotions that ripple along the cerebral neocortex found exclusively in mammalian brains. A grieving chimp or an exultant elephant is one matter, they say, but are we going to talk about jealous sponges and embarrassed mosquitoes? And of course we are not. The skein of life is a continuum, a scale encompassing higher and lower points of development, and not all creatures share the same emotional capacities. But we do not concede that feelings are limited to mammals alone. There is increasing evidence that birds, reptiles, and even fish experience some emotions. For other creatures, all we can say is that we don't yet know much and we hope one day to find out more. Even the lowly one-celled amoeba, we might point out, is known to at least avoid pain.

Finally, the dissenters decry the use of anecdotal evidence, the observations and stories that describe the existence and nature of animal emotions. Time-honored scientific method requires controlled testing and replication, they say, not merely accounts of what we see. But surely careful observation is the very foundation of sci-

ence. Darwin himself thought so; he based his most important theories on observing animals, not on controlled experiments. Simple common sense demands that we take into account what we see with our own eyes, hear with our own ears, and interpret with our own intelligence. Another time-honored staple of scientific logic is, after all, Occam's razor: The simplest explanation that covers all contingencies is probably the right one. So if a dog responds to the promise of taking a walk with alert posture, wagging tail, and enthusiastic yelps, perhaps we're not wholly off base in assuming, even asserting, that the dog is happy.

We must refine and perfect our methods of studying animals—we can and we are. But that's no reason to discard the obvious, to discount the abundant evidence of our own senses. Animal lovers know better; and the dog enthusiast or cat fancier, the fan of wildlife programs on television, might well wonder what difference it makes where science stands on the question of animal emotions. But it does matter. Science helps structure and codify our knowledge about animals—and, more important, it expands that knowledge. This is vital. The more we know about the nonhuman creatures who share our planet—and the better we both appreciate and respect their emotions—the more we will be able to live with them in civility, equity, and accord. Their world will be safer for the knowledge, and ours richer and infinitely more beautiful.

Here, then, are stories about animals' emotions, written by the people who know them best and who have devoted lifetimes to their careful study. Our authors are all scientists, eminent in their fields: animal ethologists (who investigate animals in their natural environments), behavioral ecologists (who study how animals adapt to different environments), psychologists, sociologists, and anthropologists. What follows are their observations of our fellow animals—labors of science, and labors of love.

Despite this threatening display, the gold eyelash vipers of Costa Rica's tropical rain forest are considered to be relatively mild-tempered.

LOVE

G iven its bewildering variety of forms and shadings, love is perhaps the most complex of all emotions. On this landscape where science and poetry meet, we find parental love, filial love, erotic love, romantic love, friendship, loyalty, affection, tenderness, devotion, commitment, and compassion, to name but a few.

There is considerable evidence that many nonhuman animals are capable of feelings that run the gamut of the varieties of love; in fact, it appears that some animals know more about it than we do. And the most loving creatures are not necessarily our closest animal kin.

Take, for instance, the matter of long-term loving relationships. More than 90 percent of bird species are monogamous, and in many of them the pairs mate for life. In some species, males and females form very close bonds, which yield a species-survival payoff of high reproductive success. Fewer mammals are monogamous, and the nonhuman primates appear comparatively callous when it comes to commitment: Chimpanzee males, for example, don't spend much time courting, mating, or remaining with a female whose young they've fathered. And if divorce statistics are any indication (about half the marriages in the United States dissolve), we ourselves are hardly role models of committed love.

Perhaps that's because we don't spend enough time getting to know each other, or because love's path is sometimes too smooth and easy. With animals, it's otherwise. In many species, romantic love is slow to develop between potential lovers. Males and females perform mating rituals that take much time and energy and often expose them to risk. It's as though one or both of them need to prove worthy before the relationship can be consummated.

Some animals are also adept at keeping romance alive. In monogamous species in which the same male and female breed from year to year, courtship is prolonged and vows need to be renewed. In coyotes and wolves, for example, males and females who mated previously may act like strangers the following mating season, and a new round of courtship and companionship is in order before they pair off again, rejecting all other suitors. Once their young are born they stay together, forming a true family unit, until next breeding time.

Whatever the heights and depths that romantic love inspires in individuals of any species, its overall value to nature is relentlessly purposeful: the continuation of the breed. Perhaps this is why parental love is usually an even stronger passion than the sexual variety. Many animals, human and otherwise, willingly put their own lives on the line to protect their offspring. It's hard to imagine any creature fiercer than a mother elephant or a mother bear when her young are threatened.

It's also hard to imagine anything more tender than the nurturing that many animals lavish on their babies. To begin to grasp the depth of parental love, one need only watch a gorilla mother ceaselessly grooming and cuddling her infant, or a cat bathing her newborn kittens, or whales tirelessly escorting their calves and protecting them from predators. The jaws of an alligator, which are able to bring down a deer or a man in a single crushing bite, become the gentlest of carriages when they are used to transport hatchlings safely through the water. Animal mothers and in some species fathers, older siblings, aunts, uncles, and even cousins will feed youngsters, retrieve them if they stray, patiently teach them the skills they'll need to survive. Their devotion is selfless and unflagging.

Even if love in all its forms were not manifestly obvious in many species, the latest science argues for its existence. The human mental machinery of love—the brain anatomy and the neurochemistry that allow us to feel it—is similar or identical to that of numerous other creatures. The conclusion appears inescapable: If we can know the multiform, baffling, joyous, heartbreaking, soul-stretching, and life-changing wonder of love, so can they.

NAOMI A. ROSE | *The Humane Society of the United States*

Giving a Little Latitude

Orcas are born precocious. They swim strongly immediately after birth: They literally sink or swim, in fact. They're tremendously curious as infants and juveniles. It's only with age that caution sets in. I've always found the adults conservative, preferring to avoid the unknown or the new rather than approach it rashly. But the young ones will indulge as much of their curiosity as their mothers and siblings allow.

I was observing a large group of orcas in Johnstone Strait one summer day, following them along the coast of Vancouver Island near Robson Bight. A young mother and her infant, who was perhaps only two years old, were between me and the shore. I was keeping my distance at about three hundred yards and noting their surfacings and general behaviors. Suddenly, I realized I was watching the mother surface without her calf. I looked around for the youngster; they're harder to see when they surface, since they're smaller and their breaths are rapid and indistinct. And then it became clear why I wasn't seeing him: He was right behind my boat, his head perilously close to my outboard engine's screws.

What fascinated me about this was not the calf's curiosity about my outboard. He was obviously playing, exploring his surroundings—typical mammalian infant behavior. What struck me was his mother. She'd maintained a steady distance from us while her offspring was

This mother orca and her calf, like all their kind, will probably remain inseparable. In the wild, all orca offspring share the same home range as their mothers, and male calves stay close to their mothers throughout their lives.

safely tucked at her side. Now that he insisted on examining my boat, she came nearer, overcoming her caution to stay close enough to protect him. And I was no longer following her. She was following me. The whole time the calf frolicked in my engine wash, she was a steady presence. She didn't herd him away from the potential danger; she tolerated his curiosity. But she stayed within striking distance.

Some orca mothers seem relatively tolerant of exploration in their calves; others allow their infants to move hardly more than a few feet from their side. Yet this mother indulged her offspring's playful spirit and overcame her own natural caution in order to allow him some behavioral latitude. I remember looking straight down into the calf's blowhole, he was so close to my boat, then looking up to see her dorsal fin a few yards away. She was keeping pace, keeping vigilant.

Parental love is often expressed best by allowing children to make their own mistakes and then being there to pick up the pieces and to offer support. Being overprotective is not necessarily beneficial. Perhaps some orca mothers know this, too.

RICHARD W. WRANGHAM | *Harvard University*

Making a Baby

Kakama was eight years old, on the verge of chimpanzee adolescence, but still spending most of his time alone with his mother, Kabarole, in Kibale National Park, Uganda. Kabarole was pregnant with her second child, and she slept a lot. On a typical quiet morning, while Kabarole paused for a few minutes during her walk to the next tree, Kakama tried to get a rise out of me. He stamped the ground, displaying toward me for a few steps before slapping a tree and then retreating. I sat and groomed my arm. I wanted to appear boring.

The second time he did this, Kakama somersaulted away and came to rest straddling a log. For a second he lay face down with his tummy on the log, then he continued his roll with the log held to his belly. Two more turns and he stood up, holding the end of the log with his right hand. Kabarole was already walking downslope. Kakama followed after her, dragging the log behind him as Christopher Robin did with Winnie-the-Pooh. Bump bump bump.

Kabarole led Kakama to a tree, and the pair climbed high to eat ripe fruits. The climb wasn't easy for Kakama, because he took his log with him. They visited three more trees that morning, accompanied by the log. Kakama carried it in every position imaginable—bipedal with his log on his back, cupped in two hands or held in one, tripedal with the log held by a thigh, dragged on the ground, or balanced on

the back of his neck. At one point it fell from his thirty-foot-high perch. He watched it land, and when he followed Kabarole out of the tree he immediately skipped downslope to collect his log before turning back to follow Kabarole.

The log's meaning to Kakama emerged when he made sleeping nests. His first nest was an ordinary one, in which he lay on his back with his limbs in the air, his log held over him, playing the airplane game. Just as some mothers do with their babies, Kakama slowly juggled and balanced the log above him on his four palms while he watched it.

His second nest was an odd one. It was smaller than usual and in a strange place—in the fork of a tree rather than in the comfortable outer twigs. It looked like a toy nest. After making it, he first put the log in it. He sat next to it for two minutes before climbing in himself, rather awkwardly because the nest was small.

Three years earlier, I'd seen Kakama make a small ground-nest for an unrelated one-year-old chimpanzee, carry her to it, and lay her down in it—the only time a chimpanzee has been seen to make a nest for another individual. At other times, he can spend up to an hour softly fondling and embracing an infant as he lies on his back and she crawls hesitatingly over him. Kakama is unusually drawn to the young, it seems. And when there wasn't any infant around to look after, he invented one.

Mother chimpanzees spend most of their time alone with their one or two offspring, and the youngsters often appear bored by the solitude. They perk up considerably when families meet, however; the young play rough-and-tumble games for an hour or more at a time. Kakama is shown here with one of his young friends.

ANNE RASA | *Bonn University, Germany*

A Stormy Courtship

Feral foreplay for yellow mongooses Pug and Delilah involves plenty of in-your-face mutual yowling. As legend and literature record, mongooses are as fierce in hunting as they can be in romance.

Dawn was just breaking as I slogged up the Kalahari sand dune—another day of watching my yellow mongoose (*Cynictis penicillata*) group to try and find why these solitary hunters den together and show such close social bonds. Instead of silence broken by the occasional bird's song, I was greeted by a horrendous caterwauling from underground.

My first reaction was "predator." My little group of five was being attacked! Maybe a cobra or puff adder had invaded the burrow. The godawful racket continued off and on for the next half hour, and I was on tenterhooks. The sound suggested two tomcats in combat, and I knew yellow mongooses to be usually silent, declining even to give alarm calls when they spot an enemy.

As I anxiously watched the burrow's entrance, Delilah, the dominant female, finally emerged. I expected her to bear some sign of vicious fighting, but she seemed unperturbed. She walked a little way from the burrow entrance and just sat. All was quiet underground. Then Pug, the dominant male, a battle-scarred warrior and quite the ugliest yellow mongoose of my aquaintance, trotted out and made a beeline for Delilah. Rank order fight? Expulsion from the pack? I waited for the attack, but nothing happened. Pug approached almost shyly, his head turned away. He stretched a forepaw toward Delilah, but as soon as it touched her flank, the situation exploded. She sprang to face him, screaming, and Pug replied in kind. As the two stood head to head yelling, I suddenly realized that this was the underground noise I'd heard. It wasn't fighting but love—the yellow mongooses' courtship ritual, the most raucous I've ever heard in the animal kingdom.

The mutual screaming broke off, as Delilah turned away from Pug, trotted a few steps, and sat down again. By now there was an audience: The old female Longhair; Smallears, the youngest female; and Junior, the subordinate male, had emerged from the burrow. Longhair and Smallears soon left for the day's foraging. Junior, however, was slinking around the yowling lovers, watching intently. Then Pug made a few dashes at him, and Junior also vanished into the dune grass.

The stormy courtship continued, with Pug trying to approach Delilah or block her path or trot behind her every time she moved. Each approach ended in a screaming match. This went on all day. By sunset nothing had changed, and poor Pug seemed quite exhausted.

The next dawn saw a repetition of the previous day's game, and it was late afternoon before Delilah began to thaw a little bit: She let Pug put a paw over her back. But when he tried to mount, she usually arched her back and snapped at him, and he had to jump clear. Sometimes the coy temptress actually let him mount, only to then turn on him with lunges and screeches.

The whole thing was getting rather tedious—to me, certainly, and probably to Pug. At last, just before dark, Delilah allowed her suitor the liberties he sought. In typical mon-

goose style, Pug mounted her and then pulled her backward onto his lap, where he moved her gently up and down with his forepaws. They mated several times, with much howling in between bouts, before vanishing into the burrow for the night.

The next morning Delilah emerged, first as usual, followed by a rather harassed Pug, who kept looking over his shoulder at something inside the burrow. Then the rest of the group appeared. Pug trotted toward Smallears, who screamed at him, then toward Delilah, with the same result. It was then that I realized that Smallears was also in estrus. What was Pug going to do now? The whole thing was rather comical. Poor Pug dashed from one female to the other and groomed and rubbed himself against each to a chorus of protest. He mated with Delilah several times during the morning. Meanwhile, Junior, continuing his sly patrol, was obviously waiting for his chance. While Pug was busy with one of the females, Junior would slink up and put a paw over the other. Pug would then stop what he was doing and chase Junior off before returning to business. By late afternoon, Delilah was rebutting all Pug's advances, and he was more and more attentive to Smallears.

Delilah was finally able to move off and dig out a few beetle grubs for herself (neither she nor Pug had eaten since the courtship circus began), and Junior saw his chance. He crept up and tentatively rested a paw on her back. I waited for the screams and snaps, but to my amazement, Delilah stood quietly and let Junior mate with her, not once but several times. Where was the noise and gnashing? What was going on? She and Junior continued to mate out of Pug's sight until it was dark, Delilah compliantly silent throughout.

By the next day Delilah's estrus was over and she left to forage. Now Pug could concentrate on Smallears, and the caterwauling continued for the fourth straight day, with Junior still lurking on the outskirts. Smallears violently rebuffed Pug, who—by now utterly exhausted—flopped on the sand and slept. She then held a short, quiet, but very effective tryst behind the bush with Junior.

It took me a long while to formulate a theory for the females' curious behavior, but I finally concluded that it had to do with child rearing. After the young were born, I discovered that yellow mongooses keep their young in a communal den until they're half grown. During this time, all members of the group bring food to the youngsters, after the fashion of dogs or wolves. Maybe the females' deceit—copulating with Junior and concealing it from Pug—had to do with enlisting his paternal services. Since he'd mated with both females, he might be the pups' father. He was prepared, therefore, to help supply them with food.

Whether he actually was the father of some of them I didn't know. What mattered to the group was that he thought so, and he acted accordingly.

As to the yowling storminess of the yellow mongoose courtship—unique in their generally quiet kind—I've never discovered a reasonable explanation. It remains an intriguing puzzle to be solved in the future.

The caterwauling over, Pug and Delilah consummate their passion. After the raucous preliminaries, the act itself is comparatively silent.

Marc Bekoff | *University of Colorado, Boulder*

A Nurturing Nature

Jethro came into my life at a local humane society more than a decade ago. He was about nine months old then, and he looked to be part rottweiler and part German shepherd, with a little bit of hound bobbing about in his gene pool. He was black and tan, barrel-chested, and had dripping jowls and long, floppy ears. Gentle and well mannered, my new companion didn't chase other animals at my mountain home in Boulder. He merely loved, in his laid-back way, to hang out and watch the world around him. He made a perfect field assistant for me as I studied various birds living near the house.

One day Jethro came to the front door, and instead of whining as he usually did when he wanted in, he just sat there. I saw that he carried a small, furry object in his mouth, and at first I thought he had killed a bird. But when I opened the door, Jethro dropped at my feet a very young female rabbit, drenched in his saliva but still moving. I couldn't see any injuries. I figured the helpless little ball of fur was an orphan, her mother killed by a coyote or some other predator.

When I picked her up, Jethro got very concerned. He tried to snatch her from my hands, whined, and followed me around as I gathered a box, a blanket, and some water

Good-natured Jethro likes to play with many animals, including people. He and his human companion, Marc Bekoff, particularly enjoy games of chase in a meadow near their mountain home in Colorado.

and food. I gently placed the baby rabbit in the box and wrapped her in the blanket. I decided to name her Bunny. Later I put some mashed-up carrots, celery, and lettuce near her, and she tried to eat. All the while Jethro stood behind me, panting, dripping saliva on my shoulder, and watching my every move. I thought he would go for Bunny or the food, but he just observed, fascinated by his little adoptee who was moving about in her new home.

When I had to leave the box I called Jethro, who usually came to me immediately. But he wouldn't move. He stayed steadfastly near the box for hours on end, and I finally had to drag him away for his nightly walk. When we returned he made a beeline for the box, and he slept beside it all night. I trusted him not to harm Bunny during the two weeks that I nursed her back to health, but Jethro was far more than harmless: He was protective. He was her guardian and friend.

Finally, the day came when I introduced Bunny to the outdoor world. Jethro and I walked to the east side of my house, and I released her from her box and watched her slowly make her way into a nearby woodpile. She was cautious; her senses were overwhelmed by the new sights, sounds, and odors that assailed her. Bunny stayed in the woodpile for about an hour, then she boldly stepped out to begin life as a full-fledged rabbit. Motionless,

Jethro intently watched the transformation.

Bunny hung around for a few months. Every time I let Jethro out of the house, he immediately ran to the spot where she had been released, stopping there to cock his head and wag it from side to side, looking for her. This lasted for about six months.

I'm not sure what happened to Bunny. Other rabbits, young and adult, have come and gone, and Jethro has looked at each, perhaps wondering if one were Bunny. He's always tried to get as close to them as possible, and he's never chased them.

I think Jethro is a truly compassionate soul. Last summer, nine years after he'd met Bunny and treated her with such compassion, he came running to me with another wet animal in his mouth. I asked him to drop it and he did. This time it was a young bird who'd flown into a window. It was stunned and just needed to regain its senses. I held it for a few minutes while Jethro looked on. When I thought the bird was ready to fly, I put it on the railing of my porch. Jethro approached it, sniffed it, stepped back, and watched it take wing.

Jethro has now saved two animals from death. He could thoughtlessly have gulped down either one of them with little effort. But you don't do that to friends.

Lee Alan Dugatkin | *University of Louisville*

I'll Have What She's Having

You may not know where to look for love, but evolutionary biologists do: the guppy. Native to the streams of the northern mountain ranges of Trinidad and Tobago, the little guppy (*Poecilia reticulata*), now so commonly found in pet stores, has become the proverbial white rat of animal studies of mate choice.

This is partly because guppies breed quickly and take well to the lab, and partly because—for a long time—we scientists believed that guppies were hardwired for love and that the matter of mate choice was all in their genes. Females were genetically predisposed to prefer colorful males, and that was that. When it came to courtship, every action we observed in guppies appeared to be no more than the direct and indirect effects of genes. This was, after all, a completely plausible scenario: The commands of the chromosomes dictate mate choice in many species.

As it turns out, however, this is not quite the whole story with guppies. Of course, genes play some role in guppy love. To deny this would be to fly in the face of the evidence. But a big chunk of guppy love can be explained only when we add another element: imitation. Experiments have shown that guppy females are acutely aware of what others in their school find attractive in males. In fact, when possible, female guppies copy the mate choice of those around them. It's almost as though some sort of piscine peer pressure is at work.

Cultural transmission of information regarding attractiveness is turning up more and more in animal studies of mate choice. Guppy love, however, is more than genes plus a little imitation on the side. Rather than being a secondary motivation, imitation is the primary force that drives their romantic engines. In fact, should a female see others mate with a male that possesses none of the traits she is genetically predisposed to prefer, she often chooses that male as a partner anyway. Not only that, but, at least for the immediate future, she will prefer all males who look like the choice her fellow females made. In other words, cultural transmission swamps out genetics when it comes to guppy love.

It's truly amazing that imitation plays such a large role in individuals all of one inch long, and the relative complexity of a guppy's love life has made me view the fish in a new light. It's also demonstrated to me how powerful a force cultural transmission can be. Now I can't help thinking of the almost limitless strength such a force may have in brainier animals—us, for example.

The spectacular color of male guppies such as these endears them not only to their mates but also to hobbyists who fancy tropical fish. Many aquarium keepers feed their guppies color-enhancing food that renders them even brighter.

ANNE RASA | *Bonn University, Germany*

Against All Odds

Hunters and hunted, dwarf mongooses in the wild dine on insects, snakes, eggs, and small rodents. But families must maintain a wary watch to avoid becoming meals for their own natural enemies, among them the pale chanting goshawk.

It was half past three in the afternoon in Kenya's Taru Desert and like a kiln inside the Land Cruiser. I'd been sitting there since dawn, watching the most unusual dwarf mongoose group I'd ever come across. Instead of eight to twelve adult animals, this one consisted of only two adults with two babies about three to four weeks old. I knew that normally, all the subordinate adults in the group help care for the dominant female's young, with the males standing guard and the females baby-sitting. Even then, the death toll among the youngsters is high, most of them being lost to birds of prey. How were these two, whom I called Sinbad and Sarah, going to manage to protect their babies all by themselves?

The low termite mound where the little group had slept away the heat of the day now lay partly in the welcome shade of a Commiphora tree, and within this shadow something moved. Peering through my binoculars, I could see Sinbad's head emerging from one of the termite mound's ventilation shafts. Something pushed past him and tottered to the top of the mound, where it stood blinking in the sun. It was Baby Dark-nose, one of the two youngsters, whom I could easily distinguish from its sibling, Baby Light-nose, by the darker pigment around its nostrils.

Before I could even log the time of the group's appearance, a shadow shot over the car. The next thing I saw was a pale chanting goshawk diving at the baby and grabbing it in its talons. The hawk's trajectory carried it about five yards away from the mound, where it landed with a thump in the grass, the baby still grasped in its claws. Then the hawk began to feed. I saw it lower its head and pull at the carcass, tear something off, and swallow it.

Within a spilt second of the attack, Sinbad and Sarah were standing shoulder to shoulder on the mound. Then, their hair standing on end like bottlebrushes, they charged the hawk at full gallop. Sinbad's front feet connected with the hawk's breast, and the little mongoose's momentum was more than enough to knock the much bigger bird onto its back, with its wings spread in an attempt to keep its balance. As Sinbad hit the hawk, Sarah snapped at the gaping yellow beak above her head, then the two mongooses turned and ran back to the termite mound.

In the press of bodies on the mound, it took me a while to realize that where two had left, three had returned. Sinbad and Sarah, through their almost suicidal charge, had managed to rescue Baby Dark-nose. He was now even easier to identify than before: His tail was missing. This was the part I'd seen the hawk bite off and swallow. Aside from this amputa-

tion, however, he seemed undamaged. Sarah quickly grabbed him by the scruff of the neck and disappeared with him into the mound, closely followed by Baby Light-nose. Sinbad remained outside, making loud warning calls at the rather confused and rumpled hawk until it finally took off and vanished among the trees.

Although I was to see several such success-ful rescue attempts in future years, none remains as vivid in my memory as this particu-lar incident. In all the others, the whole pack attacked a bird that was too slow to get off the ground with its prey, and the chances of a sin-gle animal being hurt was low. That Sinbad and Sarah had hurled themselves all alone at a potentially lethal opponent in order to save their baby was one of the bravest things I'd ever seen these little mongooses do.

But their triumph was short-lived. Despite all their parents' care, the two babies didn't sur-vive their first ten days on the surface. One after the other, they were killed and carried off by hungry birds of prey. Against so many ene-mies, two parents, no matter how devoted, were simply not enough.

DAVID MACDONALD | *Oxford University and Cornell University*

Night School

This red fox cub seems to regard parental grooming as an invitation to play. With mother or father in close attendance, young foxes begin exploring outside their dens when they're about a month old. The pups usually number four or five to a litter and are cared for by both parents.

In the 1970s, I was lucky to come by the hot eye, a pair of infrared binoculars that revolutionized my study of red foxes. In particular, and unexpectedly, I discovered that foxes foraging on lush Oxfordshire pastures were far from the rapacious hunters of rural folklore; rather, much of their food came in the surprising form of the earthworm, *Lumbricus terrestis.* These earthworms, as every fisherman knows, crawl to the surface when the weather is right. On still, warm nights, in their quest for delights of the flesh and the occasional moldy leaf, some slither unprotected through the jungle of grass; others, perhaps of lesser mettle or greater prudence, retain a toehold in the soil, with tails anchored and chaetae well dug in. On nights when the worms are up, foxes meander slowly but purposefully across the fields.

There's great precision in a fox's pursuit of worms. Each fur-padded footfall follows a measured pace. Long pauses punctuate the quest, while the fox, with head cocked and ears perked, struggles to listen over the din of rustling leaves. Suddenly, the fox freezes, brush poker-stiff, ears flicking. Below its snout, an amorous pair of worms have incautiously rasped their chaetae on the grass in a moment of hermaphrodite rapture. The fox's snout points like a laser at the noisy indiscretion and plunges into the grass. Too late the unfortunate couple disentangle from their mucilaginous

47

embrace, and one finds its head neatly clamped between the fox's incisors, its tail wedged safe in its burrow. Skillfully, the fox avoids snapping its victim. Rather it pauses, holding the worm momentarily taut before raising its muzzle in an arc, slowly at first but accelerating as the prey is drawn smoothly and intact from its sanctuary. Flinging itself into contortions, the earthworm winds around the fox's muzzle, but the captor, its jaws maneuvering with the dexterity of an Italian's fork, deftly slips this animated spaghetti down the chute.

One moonless night, I stalked across a favored worming pasture with the hot eye. After many minutes of silent footsteps, I reached a ridge, raised the binoculars, and peered over. There I saw Toothypeg standing not thirty meters from me, accompanied by her leggy cub. Toothypeg, so called because only one worn canine tooth remained in her antique muzzle, was my oldest radio-collared fox, then approaching her ninth birthday.

It was the first time I'd seen that cub away from its den. It had rained heavily that afternoon, and the grass was still moist. The air was so still that even I could hear the rasping of worms on the move. The old vixen paced silently to and fro, pausing, pinpointing the grating of worm bristles on grass, stabbing her nose into the sward. Thrashing wildly, worm after worm wrapped itself around her snout. Once, when she caught a worm, the cub ran to investigate. In his gangling youthfulness he, too, had been trying to catch worms, leaping high into the air and thudding down on them with

outstretched forepaws. Pouncing with this characteristic leap may be ideal for pulverizing wood mice, but applied to these slippery delicacies, the technique left the cub biting at his feet as the worm slithered unharmed under his toes.

The cub turned his attention to Toothypeg, and within seconds she caught another worm. This one had its tail firmly anchored. Instead of drawing her prize clear of its burrow, the old vixen held it taut until her frolicking offspring summoned the temerity to take hold of it gingerly. With an incompetent tug, he snapped the worm in two and clacked his teeth noisily on the gritty morsel. Methodically the vixen caught another, again held it taught, and let the cub take it, but once more he fumbled. But now she had his full attention. As she searched, he was at her side, his nose tracing the same course as hers.

The next worm was so well lodged in its burrow that Toothypeg could barely grip it. Normally she might have cut her losses, rewarding such annelid obstinacy with a body-snapping flick. But now she paused, holding the tip of the worm in her front teeth while the cub excitedly sniffed her muzzle. Astonishingly, Toothypeg began to tap her captive gently with her forepaw. The worm heaved valiantly in its mortal tug-of-war, pinioned and pulled by an adversary some thousand-fold its weight. At first only a paw's width of worm was free from the soil, and it seemed that its injuries might be limited to the amputation of a few replaceable segments. But Toothypeg's hypnotic massage was irresistible; again and again, she gently brought her paw up to stroke at the straining sliver of life. Ten seconds edged by. Caressed

like a guitar string, the worm began to weaken its hold on its burrow. Bit by bit the vixen patted it free, until, vanquished, it was two-thirds drawn from the ground. She held it for the cub to snatch greedily.

His appetite whetted, the cub redoubled his efforts to capture a worm of his own. But he was transformed: Gone was the previous infantile bungling. True, he still caught nothing, but in a few short minutes he had learned the principle—inept maybe, but now he foraged with the adult style.

Several days later, I saw Toothypeg and her cub again. Experience still weighed in the old vixen's favor; she caught four worms each minute to her cub's one. But by the time our paths crossed again a month later, he'd graduated with distinction and was catching as proficiently as his mother. It's an observation I've never repeated, but it was sufficient to convince me that worm-catching for foxes is culture passed on from mother to cub.

CARRON A. MEANEY | *Denver Museum of Natural History*

In Perfect Unison

Pals and partners Turbo and Kachina team up for a cross-country marathon. These five- to ten-kilometer races test the horses' fearlessness, agility, and stamina. Turbo and Kachina seem to enjoy them, celebrating with elaborate post-race nudging.

Turbo and Kachina are a matched pair of gray Arabian horses. They've been stablemates and partners for more than ten years now. Turbo is strong, solid, friendly, outgoing, and doesn't scare easily. Kachina is gentle, sweet, easy—and sometimes skittish. With Turbo at her side, she can face anything. By herself, however, she's shy and nervous. If her partner is absent during a trail ride, she refuses to cross such obstacles as creeks and bridges.

The bond between the two horses formed as they learned to work together at a horse ranch outside of Boulder, pulling a cart for cross-country competitions. It took a while for them to ease into the partnership, to learn to move smoothly and without jostling each other. At first each followed its own rhythm, pushing and pulling against the other. In time, though, they learned to move in perfect unison. In the hazards part of cross-country courses, Turbo and Kachina pull the cart at breakneck speed through water obstacles, barreling around a pole in the middle of foot-deep water, flying through gates at right-angle turns with only inches to spare. They run with shared excitement and enthusiasm.

With partnership has come a deep attachment. They depend on each other, and they get upset when they're separated. When one is being loaded into a trailer while the other waits its turn, they nicker back and forth to each other constantly until both are inside. Once, at a competition in another county, the horses were spending the night together in an outdoor paddock. In the middle of the night it began to storm, and we moved them into adjacent stalls in the barn. Although warm and dry, they couldn't see each other. Clearly agitated, they whinnied back and forth throughout the night. It seemed that they preferred to face the storm together rather than be housed in comfort apart.

Sometimes I ride Turbo in the ring near their paddocks. Kachina is left behind. Each time we ride near her she whinnies for him, as if to say, "What are you doing out there without me?" When both are being ridden and Kachina finishes first and leaves the arena, Turbo pulls and strains at the bridle to join her. It's as though the two horses have formed a single personality over the years, with each constituent part incomplete without the other.

Surely this is a form of love.

ALEXANDER SKUTCH | *Costa Rica*

Singing the Praises of Family

For six decades I've studied the birds that live year-round in tropical America, and I have found that when it comes to mating, they're a pretty dull lot. Courtship is unspectacular and coition is perfunctory. But if they are short on romance, some of these birds are long on fidelity: Sometimes, when only a few months old, they form pairs that may endure as long as both members survive.

Uninspired lovers, the tropical American birds nevertheless seem to be fairly passionate parents. The most emotionally charged moments for a long-mated pair breeding undisturbed are the critical points of a nesting cycle: choosing the nest site, hatching the eggs, and the nestlings' departures.

On several mornings, a male garden thrush (*Turdus grayi*) sang in a shrub in front of our dining room window, persuading his mate to build her nest there. A male scarlet-rumped tanager (*Ramphocelus passerinii*) came repeatedly to sing in a bush beside my study, calling his partner, who built her nest in the spot he'd chosen. Seeking a nest site, a pair of gray-capped flycatchers (*Myiozetetes granadensis*) often seem to consult together. Probably the female chooses the spot, while her interested partner attends her closely. The nest song of one flycatcher stimulates the others to murmur softly. I've

seen gray-caps and related vermilion-crowned flycatchers (*M. similis*) sing this way while testing nest sites. In neighboring orange trees, on one occasion, a male boat-billed flycatcher (*Megarhynchus pitangua*) sat in the nest his mate was building and twittered softly as she perched nearby holding a stick for the structure. While they incubate eggs or brood nestlings, flycatchers often sing in undertones. Songbirds (oscines) may sing loudly while they incubate. For many birds, incubation appears to be more than stolid, unemotional sitting.

Stronger emotion is stirred by hatching eggs. A small grayish flycatcher—disparagingly called paltry tyrannulet (*Zimmerius vilissimus*) by ornithologists who don't know it well, but mistletoe flycatcher by its friends—built a cozy nest with a side entrance in a flowering shrub. To learn whether her eggs had hatched, I set a ladder below the nest one afternoon and climbed up. She was clinging in the doorway, vocalizing softly. She'd been so absorbed by a hatching egg, and I by adjusting my ladder, that each of us remained unaware of the other until my head was high enough to see her. She promptly flew out to protest the intrusion.

Sitting in her open cup at daybreak one April day with a newborn nestling and a hatching egg beneath her, a lesser elaenia (*Elaenia chiriquensis*) repeated for many minutes a simplified version of her mate's dawn song. *De weet, de*

weet, she sang in a queer, dry voice. During the fortnight that she had incubated in a rose-apple tree near an open window, I had not heard her make such sounds, which I had believed were confined to males. The birth of a nestling stirred her to utter notes she seldom used.

The fledgings' leaving the nest is the third event that prompts strong parental feelings. Returning with insects in her bill, a vermilion-crowned flycatcher found that a nestling who had lingered exceptionally long in the nest had finally flown in her absence. For many minutes she repeated soft notes much like her nest song, at first while alone, then after she'd joined her fledgling in a nearby tree.

One of the most impressive celebrations of a nestling's graduation that I've witnessed was by a pair of pale-headed jacamars *(Brachy-galba goeringi)* in Venezuela. While I stood beside a rural road, a fledgling emerged from a long burrow in the steep bank below me and rose to a tree, where both parents promptly joined it and started to sing. Each crescendo of weets and twitters preceded a high, thin trill. With variations, they repeated this song again and again while they turned from side to side and twitched their tails rapidly up and down, beating time to their animated notes. At intervals the fledgling joined its parents with its weaker voice. For a long while the trio continued to sing what impressed me as a triumphant paean for the successful conclusion of their nesting.

Christine Drea and her friend Phoenix share an affectionate moment. Although they can be lovably doglike, hyenas are not, in fact, canids, members of the dog family. They're in a class by themselves—the Hyaenidae—and their closest cousins aren't dogs but mongooses and meerkats.

Christine Drea | *Duke University*

There, There

Spotted hyenas are probably not the first animals that come to mind when we think of emotion, especially not if the feeling in question reflects a soft side. After all, we wouldn't expect such a fiercely aggressive species to experience fear or need reassurance, maternal tenderness, or sympathy. But after many years working with captive spotted hyenas at the University of California, Berkeley, I find that they're precisely the animals that come to mind when I ponder the issue of animal emotion. I've witnessed various hyenas behaving in ways that might suggest affection, spite, or even jealousy, but one particular animal stands out in his exhibiting of anguish and insecurity.

Through the course of a naturally difficult delivery, our hero had been severely deprived of oxygen at birth, and without medical intervention, he would have faced certain death. So we removed him from his mother, resuscitated him, warmed him, coddled him, and subsequently hand-reared him. Since he'd metaphorically risen from ashes, the name Phoenix seemed appropriate.

One of his brothers had been stillborn; the other, Cahli, was healthy, feisty, and thriving under his mother's care. But Phoenix spent most of his infancy in my office, tugging at shoelaces, attacking stuffed toys, demanding attention, whining for milk, and generally being

55

a pesky, though adorable, troublemaker. He did spend some time with his sibling, learning the often-harsh rules of hyena social conduct. Eventually, Phoenix was weaned from bottles and gradually transitioned out of human quarters and into hyena ones.

I visited him often. Calling his name from a distance would start a cascade of hyena vocalizations, from eager whoops to baby squitters (pig-like squeals) to incessant whines (pathetic attempts at begging, no doubt). He would fold his ears down, pull his lips back in a characteristic grin, and generally carry on the way a cub does with its mother. He'd scarcely wait for me to enter his pen before attempting a proper hyena greeting, with raised leg, but he'd usually crumble to the floor in his excitement. Once the official salute was over, he'd stand up and begin an intense investigation of my face, smelling every inch of skin. He relished eyebrows and eyelashes and would groom them attentively with his sandpaper tongue, bringing new meaning to the term "exfoliation." The smell of hair conditioner or deodorant would send him into a frenzy of rubbing. Even as a youngster, he'd press his cheek and neck up against me with enough force to topple me over. His routine invariably included a flurry of play, with Phoenix either running in circles with reckless abandon or plowing into me,

Cuddly as a puppy, Phoenix nuzzles Drea during a playful interlude. But while hyenas can and sometimes do bond with humans, they fare best in the wild.

scoring extra points for knockdowns. Eventually, he'd wear himself out, settle down in my lap, and relax while I tickled his tummy. Needless to say, our time together was serious work, all for the advancement of science.

A few years later, when Phoenix was a young adult, he and Cahli had an unfortunate encounter with some seasoned female "bruisers." Our boys were growing up and finally experiencing firsthand the misery of being male in female-dominated hyena society. I arrived at work to a parking lot packed with vans and veterinary personnel and immediately had a sinking feeling. Cahli was already being tended to—his wounds required stitches—but it was harder to determine the extent of Phoenix's injuries or even if he needed to be sedated. I rushed to his pen to find several people trying unsuccessfully to calm him down. He was inconsolable and simply would not stop pacing long enough to allow anyone to look him over.

The words "How is he?" barely passed my lips, but they were enough to bring Phoenix to a standstill. Pacing was replaced with an outpouring of pitiful whining. He met me at the fence, falling to his carpels and continuing with his cacophony, as though recounting the morning's ordeal. His body posture epitomized hyena submissiveness—bared teeth in an open-mouthed appeasement grin, ears plastered to his head, the look of defeat in his stance. As I entered his pen, he glued himself to me. If he could have jumped into my arms at that moment, he probably would have. Instead, his hindquarters turned to jelly, he sank to the floor, and like any frightened creature, he relieved himself all over my boots.

With Phoenix entwined with my legs, I stumbled to a pile of straw and sat down. Before I was even fully seated, he crawled into my lap (which he'd long since outgrown), turned over on his back, stared up at me with bewildered eyes, and whined a little longer, as if to add a plaintive postscript. As I consoled him and checked for cuts, he lowered his head, closed his eyes, and fell sound asleep.

Granted, Phoenix had taken an emotional beating, but there was hardly a physical bruise on him. A little disinfectant here, a little patting there, and he was good to go. In scientific terms, he was a low-ranking hyena who had suffered the stress and acute changes in circulating cortisol concentrations brought on by social interactions with higher-ranking animals. In layman's terms, he was merely a frightened hyena who needed comforting.

JAAK PANKSEPP | *Bowling Green State University*

The Chemistry of Caring

For as long as I can remember, the prevailing opinion in my scientific specialty (behavioral neuroscience) has been that animals feel no emotions. More recently, this arrogant position has marginally mellowed. Now the popular position is that we will never really know whether they do feel emotions or not; hence it's not a relevant scientific issue.

I beg to disagree. Even though there are substantial difficulties in scientifically studying the brain's ancient processes, there's overwhelming evidence that other mammals have many of the same basic emotional circuits that we do. And to all appearances, they have the same feelings. I can only assume that skeptics who still believe that animals are emotionally comatose zombies are succumbing to sixteenth-century thinking. Or perhaps they've had too little direct experience with the animals about which they opine. Anyone who's spent much quality, hands-on time with other mammals knows how unwarranted is the assumption that they have no feelings. I know this from the animals I've studied—and the animals I've lived with.

My favorite pet story concerns a time a quarter century ago when our two unfixed female cats, a matron and her daughter, got pregnant about the same time. Toward the end of gestation, they built nests in closets on opposite ends of our long, ranch-style home. The mother gave birth first, showering her abundant feline affections on her four kittens. The daughter, about to give birth for the first time, also became filled with maternal desire. A few days before having her own litter, the daughter cat took charge of her mother's brood, carrying the kittens to her own nest. Then we had a few days of chaos, as mother and daughter repeatedly ferried the kittens between their two domains. Nature clearly prepares such instinctual tendencies, of which caring feelings are part and parcel, through neural and hormonal changes that occur a few days before the birth process begins.

Obviously, nurturant urges are remarkably robust in all mammalian mothers (and at times in fathers), and we're even beginning to understand exactly where and how affectionate mother-infant bonds take shape within the brain. When this attachment bond is broken by separation, the mother's distress is intense, and the kittens' responses verge on panic. They cry constantly and pitiably, which helps inform their mothers of their whereabouts.

We know many of the neurochemistries that activate these strong feelings and expressions of loss—the primordial evolutionary sources of separation distress in all animals. We also know the chemistries that soothe such

Basic transportation for an infant kitten comes from its mother's gentle jaws. Kitten-toting and other maternal feline behaviors are activated by certain brain chemicals that also prompt the manufacture and release of milk for nursing.

awful feelings during the relief of reunion. These are probably the same chemistries that create our own social bonds and our feelings of love and devotion and those of despair when bonds are severed.

The feelings that result from social loss eventually lead to depression if separation is too prolonged. Drugs that alleviate these feelings are currently being used to treat pets who exhibit persistent emotional distress when their owners are away. They are the same agents that can alleviate human emotional anguish and despair, indicating once more that we do share fundamentally similar emotional systems and affective experiences with many other creatures of the world. Indeed, the evidence is now inescapable: At the basic emotional level, all mammals are remarkably similar.

ANNE BEKOFF | *University of Colorado, Boulder*

In Sickness and in Health

An old mated pair, malamutes Kobuk and Tika have settled into comfy domesticity. Here Tika rests peacefully as Kobuk grooms her right ear.

Over the years, Kobuk and Tika had settled into a comfortable pattern. As a breeding pair of champion malamute show dogs, they had raised eight litters of puppies together and now they were enjoying their golden years with me in Boulder, Colorado.

Kobuk was the charming, energetic, outgoing one, very demanding of attention. You always knew when his ears needed rubbing or his belly needed scratching—or when he was hungry or had to go outside. Then he bounced and pranced and enthusiastically leaned into you until you gave in. As a typical malamute, he was quite vocal, woo-wooing his way into everyone's heart. Tika, on the other hand, was quieter and stayed in the background most of the time. You really couldn't get much of a sense of her personality, except that she had a very sweet face. If anyone tried to pay attention to Tika's ears or belly, Kobuk would shove in between and insisted that his needs were far more important than hers. Tika knew not to eat her food unless it was a safe distance from his. At walk time, Kobuk always got to go through the doorway first. If Tika happened to be in the way, she was likely to get knocked over as he exploded past her.

Like any long-married couple, Kobuk and Tika had worked out ways of settling their differences. If sufficiently upset, Kobuk would attack Tika, biting her neck and growling fiercely until you were sure she was going to be seriously injured, if not killed. Remarkably, she always survived, no blood was ever seen, and the attacks were short-lived: After them, both dogs behaved as though nothing unusual had happened. Still, it was disturbing to witness such episodes. They made you wonder how close the two dogs really were.

One day a small lump appeared on Tika's leg. It quickly grew larger, ulcerated the skin, and was diagnosed as a malignant tumor. Overnight, Kobuk's behavior changed. He became quite subdued. He wanted to stay right by his mate's side, even when there were people around. He spent his time watching her or gently grooming her ears and face. He didn't get in the way when she needed her bandages changed. After she had her leg amputated and was having trouble getting around, I could always tell when I came home if she had fallen and hurt herself. Kobuk would be lying in his kennel looking very worried; he wouldn't even get up to greet me. It was as though he felt guilty for her pain. He no longer shoved past her to get through doorways or up stairs. He didn't even mind when she was allowed to get on the bed without him.

About two weeks after Tika's surgery, Kobuk woke me up in the middle of the night the way he does when he really needs to go outside. Tika was in another room of the house, and Kobuk ran over to her; so I got her up, too, and took them outside. But strangely, both of them just lay down on the grass. Only then did I first hear Tika's very soft whining. Puzzled, I brought them back inside, where I saw that Tika's belly was huge and swollen. She was going into shock by the time I got her to the emergency veterinary clinic, but they were able to save her life. If Kobuk hadn't fetched me from sleep, Tika almost certainly would have died before I realized anything was wrong.

Gradually, Tika recovered from her two surgeries. As she regained her health and learned to maneuver on three legs, Kobuk began to relax. Soon he was transformed back into the rambunctious, attention-seeking charmer he'd been before. The only difference is that now I know, as Tika has always known, that Kobuk will be there for her when it counts.

Bernd Würsig | *Texas A&M University*

Leviathan Love

When bowhead, gray, and right whales mate, the process usually involves one female (apparently reluctant) and an entourage of males (eager and boisterous). The female turns her belly to the surface for many minutes, punctuated only by her need to breathe, at which time she rapidly turns, races off, blows several times, and then rolls belly-up again. The jostling males try to roll her back-up so they can mate from below, or to align their own bellies so that their long, muscular penises can snake over from their bodies to hers. Researchers are now certain that females in estrous mate with several males and that the males practice "sperm competition," pumping huge volumes of sperm into the females to flood out or at least dilute the contributions of others. That's why these whales have the largest testicles per body size of any marine mammals. Statistically, the male with the most sperm in the most females will sire the most offspring, his genetic ticket to the future.

At the same time, the female may be practicing a form of partner choice by making insemination difficult. Presumably, only the strongest or most agile and tenacious male gets to mate with her. His prowess will devolve on her young, so her genes, too, will have greater success over the ages.

This is all fine and good; and a mating group with one whale belly-up, a boil of white water, and an array of large, pink penises is a

The head of a male right whale nudges the side of another, most likely a female, in an apparent attempt to push or roll her into mating position.

common sight for those of us who investigate these marvelously strange creatures. The activity may be structured, but it looks to us like a disorganized mess, devoid of emotional attachment and certainly of love.

However, I have seen a different mating sequence—only once, but very clearly. It happened in the austral winter of 1974 while I stood on a cliff overlooking southern right whales (*Eubalaena australis*) at their mating/calving grounds on the Valdés Peninsula in Argentina. Sunrise revealed a group of three whales near the foot of the cliff, vivid against a calm, flat sea. The female was in classic belly-up position, and one large and one slightly smaller male were circling, nudging her, perhaps gauging how best to approach. I'll call the female Aphrodite, Aphro for short, and the males Butch and Shrimp.

The males repeatedly stationed themselves belly-up on either side of Aphro, and I could see their tapered penises unsheathe from their genital slits and feel their way along Aphro's belly. Each time this happened, she would displace the males by surging forward, turning up to blow several times, racing ahead for two or three whale lengths, then resuming her belly-up posture, as if to say, "I'm simply not interested." All this was normal enough; I had seen it many times before.

After about an hour, however, both penises managed to find Aphro's genital slit and snake inside. This was a new sight for me: Aphro sandwiched between Butch and Shrimp

and connected to both of them by pink funnels, one slightly smaller than the other. Because of the belly-up postures, the penises couldn't fully insert, despite the males' attempts to lean in as much as possible. Remarkably, after two minutes of this dual partial insertion, Aphro began to lean her own body toward Butch, so that she effectively pulled Shrimp's appendage out of her. She remained belly-up, however, as did Butch. His right pectoral flipper slid under the insertion point of her left one, so that the two whales were stabilizing each other by—in effect—holding hands.

It seemed to me that Aphro had clearly chosen her preferred mate; Shrimp quickly swam away and began to breach and tail slap—typical behavior of a "loser" male, possibly signaling anger or frustration.

Aphro and Butch now moved slowly, with no white water, no boisterous activity. If a combined mass of one hundred tons of whale can be called tender, these two were being tender; holding onto each other as they rocked sideways, almost imperceptibly, toward and away, toward and away. After about two minutes of this, with perhaps three feet of Butch's penis inserted and another three or four feet in air, I saw muscle contractions begin at the base of his penis and glide in a gentle, circular wave toward Aphro and into her. Within four or five seconds there were six such waves, which presumably deposited Butch's sperm. Moments after the contractions stopped, Butch's penis grew smaller and flopped along Aphro's belly before retracting into its own genital slit.

What happened next is perhaps the most significant element of the tale. Aphro and Butch

Right whales have very long penises in order to reach the female. This whale's penis is partially extended during part of a mating sequence.

64

didn't separate and swim off, as I'd expected. Instead, they continued to touch flippers, beginning a slow caressing motion that lasted about twenty seconds. Then they rolled toward each other, briefly locking both sets of flippers in a sort of hug before rolling back to lie side by side, blowing for perhaps three minutes more. They left the cliffs at a leisurely pace, swimming close together, touching, surfacing, and diving in unison. I watched the two of them for another hour or so before they slipped into an adjacent bay and out of my sight.

We behavioral researchers should probably call this event a mere example of an "alternative mating strategy" and perhaps speculate that it deviated from the norm only because there were few males in the immediate area. Perhaps Aphro simply got tired of making life difficult for an ardent suitor and decided to save her energy by acquiescing to his attentions. Perhaps Butch stayed with Aphro after mating in order to protect his investment of sperm.

I prefer to think, however, that the two became powerfully attracted to each other and had at least a feeling of afterglow as they swam off. Butch and Aphro were the "right" right whales for each other. I don't know how long they stayed together or whether they mated again. But for them, could it not have been love?

LEE ALAN DUGATKIN | *University of Louisville*

Risking It All for Love

The most colorful of male guppies put themselves at risk and call attention to themselves by inspecting potential predators, but only when there's a female audience. In the absence of females, the most colorful males don't indulge in inspection behavior any more often than the drabber males.

A rather odd spectacle occurs when a school of guppies (*Poecilia reticulata*) spots a potential predator. Rather than every fish swimming for the nearest hiding place, certain individuals—the "inspectors"—actually move away from the safety of the group and toward the predator. This is truly a sight to behold. These fearless fish risk life and limb to gather information about a threat facing every member of their group. If that isn't enough, inspectors then somehow share their knowledge with the guppies who stay back and don't assume any of the risks.

After the wonder of viewing inspection behavior for the first time wears off, some obvious questions arise: How could such bold, risk-taking behavior ever evolve? Why doesn't natural selection slowly decrease the numbers of fearless fish? The answer, naturally, lies in a thorough understanding of the costs and benefits of inspecting versus not inspecting. Since most of the work on this question has focused on males, we'll limit our discussion to this sex.

First, let's consider the cost of being a bold fish versus the security of being an anxious (noninspecting) fish. If you put bold and anxious males together with a potential predator, what happens? Risk takers do what comes naturally: They inspect, and in the end a greater proportion of them end up in the stomach of the predator. Clearly, fearless fish pay for their courage. But what, if anything, do they get in

return? The answer is a better love life. Risk-taking males are viewed by females as more attractive, more suitable mates than are their anxious groupmates.

Experimental work has uncovered a fascinating interaction between boldness, color, and attractiveness in guppies. We now know that the more colorful males are the ones more likely to inspect predators. It has also been shown that differences in inspection behavior between the brave, colorful male guppies and the drab, fearful ones appear only when females are watching. In other words, there's no difference in the way all male guppies behave in the presence of a predator unless they know they have a female audience. We've seen that the female guppies prefer colorful, venturesome males as potential mates. Interestingly, though, when color and boldness are experimentally uncoupled, it turns out that the male's boldness—not his color—is what makes him attractive to females. Therefore, one clear evolutionary benefit to being an inspector male guppy is that (presuming you survive your daring behavior) you're much more alluring as a sexual partner.

As a behavioral ecologist, I'm obliged to think about the costs and benefits of inspection in order to piece together its evolution and maintenance. That being said, though, merely watching the equivalent of sentry duty unfold in fish with brains barely larger than pencil points is in itself a breathtaking experience.

JOHN C. FENTRESS | *Dalhousie University, Nova Scotia, and the University of Oregon*

Lessons of the Heart

Much of what I know about passion in animals I learned from my first wolf. His name was Lupey. I acquired him as a pup from the Whipsnade Zoo outside London. I was a research student at Cambridge. I loved him, and he loved me. We shared a passion.

The idea of acquiring a wolf raised eyebrows: My student journal recorded the comments from a thesis coadvisor. "Let's see," he said. "What you are asking is for us to give you our land, to keep your pets, which are potentially dangerous, at our expense, to support a hobby that will take time from your research, a project that may well fail. Is that right?"

"Yes," I responded.

"Seems reasonable enough," he said.

So it began. Being enthusiastically true to oneself is perhaps a reasonable synonym for passion. Lupey showed me some of his passion, as well as his compassion. The latter implies sharing. Passion included Lupey's insistence on being himself, a wolf, even though reared under strange circumstances. Our first night at Cambridge was hard. He howled in my bedroom, but when I brought him onto my bed he snuggled under my pillow and slept soundly much of the rest of the night. By the next morning he was following me around the house.

Lupey's passion for play was soon evident. He played games that ranged from "pull the

Lupey plays "pull on the hat" in the mid-sixties with research student John Fentress, a favorite game that enhanced their friendship, if not Fentress's wardrobe. According to Fentress, wolves love games that involve tugging and pulling.

69

towel" and "eat the books" to our own version of rugby (which he always won). And there were other passions. He expressed anger at my missteps in our relationship but was always forgiving if he felt I'd made these errors out of simple human stupidity. Sometimes he was willful. He tried to dig through the wall of my bedroom and couldn't be stopped. He insisted on doing what he wanted, yet through the years he also grew sensitive to what I wanted him to do, and he shared in my expectations for him.

Let me tell two stories that reflect the internal framework within which he operated.

One day, while Lupey and I were staying on a farm in Cambridgeshire, I stepped outside to see my friend and he startled me with a loud snarl. I stepped back. He wagged his tail and gave those wonderful, welcoming, wolf squeaking sounds. I stepped forward again, to be greeted with a second snarl, louder and longer than the first. I stepped back and was favored with tail wags and squeaks. We repeated this dance several times.

Lupey clearly was not expressing a dislike for me in general, but for something I was inadvertently doing. It turned out that when I stepped forward, I stood on chicken parts that he'd buried. Snarls. I stepped back off this hidden chicken. Squeaks and wags. Lesson One: Don't stand on a wolf's chicken. Lesson Two: If it's an honest mistake, it's OK. My impression was that he understood I had no malign intent. I suspect wolves are sophisticated enough to respond not just to actions but also to their own interpretations of them. This implies more

The young Lupey enjoyed blankets, both for comfort and for gnawing. "Many blankets had many holes," says Fentress, "and each hole remains a treasure."

than passion in expression; it approaches what child psychologists call a "theory of mind."

The second story:

At a kennel in Rochester, New York, one of the dog caretakers got impatient because Lupey was slow to leave his indoor den area for the outside pen, connected by a flap door. I wasn't there at the time, but I saw the consequences. This person, whom Lupey normally treated with his typical enthusiasm, hit the wolf on the head with a shovel. By the time I arrived, Lupey was standing on his hind legs, snarling into the man's face. Several of us worked together to get the caretaker out of the enclosure. I went back into the pen with Lupey, but with reservations; after all, he could have decided that people—all people—were not his companions at all. But he wagged his tail and squeaked. We then had several other adults enter the pen, and finally a four-year-old girl, accompanied by her father. In each case Lupey was his usual friendly self.

The shovel-man was then invited back. At once, Lupey was on his hind legs again, snarling into the man's face. We repeated the exercise the next day, and for several days over the next three weeks. The offending caretaker could never again enter Lupey's area. All other visitors were enthusiastically welcomed.

There are both contrasts and commonalities in the two stories. In the chicken story, somebody acted stupidly (wolf language) but innocently. There was no harm intended. But a rule had been broken, and in some respects Lupey treated me the way adults might treat a small child: Acknowledge and act on the breaking of the rule, but don't generalize as to the

character of the child. In short, do not withdraw your love. Compartmentalize. In the shovel story, something very different occurred. "This man" (reading Lupey's notes) "intentionally acted in a way that could harm me. I cut him off forever! I can no longer trust him. But there are many others whom I trust, and my relations with them are basically unchanged." Compartmentalize.

This means, I believe, that wolves can indeed do much more than respond to overt actions. I stepped on a chicken; I was merely innocently stupid. The other man was intentionally aggressive—an enemy. In each case the wolf compartmentalized, but by different rules: a warning, but with no withdrawal of love, in response to innocent stupidity; aggression, specifically directed, toward a man who'd displayed hostile intent.

Obviously, such observations are anecdotal and are prone to individual human interpretation. But the incidents convinced me. I am sure that wolves have rich and sophisticated inner lives that get sorted out in wolf ways, passionate and compassionate.

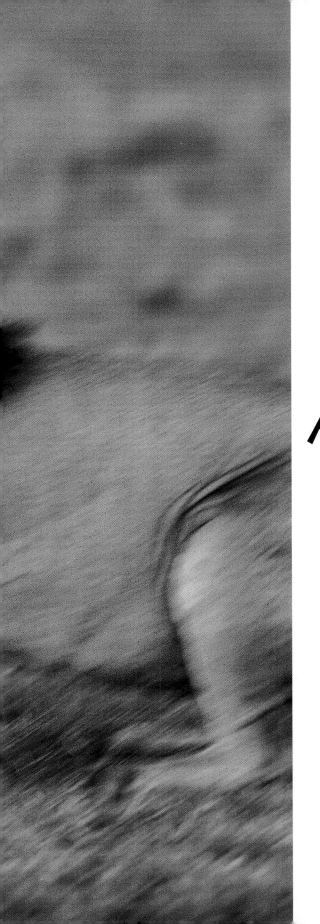

FEAR,
AGGRESSION,
AND ANGER

I f love is the most convoluted of emotions, fear is probably the most straightforward. It's a feeling shared by almost all animals, from reptiles to humans, and
necessarily so: Knowing when to be afraid is crucial for survival.

Scientists refer to fear as a primary emotion, meaning that it is basic, hardwired to an evolutionarily old part of the brain. Secondary emotions—love or
grief, for instance, or embarrassment or compassion—involve nuance and degree and
usually entail conscious thought. But fear exists on a different level. Primal and
direct, utterly unsubtle, it's the armament without which no individual or species will
survive. Faced with a swooping hawk or stalking leopard, the potential prey has no
time to think. It must react—correctly and the first time—or die.

Reactions to fear are usually obvious. An animal faced with a threatening stimulus may cower, run, or become combative, as instantaneous neural- and hormone-
driven changes in heart rate, blood flow, and body temperature prepare it to either
defend itself or get away—the well-known "fight or flight" response. Some animals
react by becoming motionless, since movement can draw attention.

Among fearful stimuli are heights, large shapes, specific odors, and certain
sounds. Not all animals react to the same ones or in the same ways. In some mice
and rats, for example, a moderately fearsome stimulus causes them to freeze, while a
more potent danger makes them run.

Whatever the response, however, fear is clearly instinctive. Laboratory rats who
have never encountered cats nevertheless freeze in response to their smell. A stimulus
as innocuous as cat hair can make them anxious. In fact, some animals show fear even
before birth: In certain bird species, raucous sounds can bring the movements of
late-term embryos to a halt, arresting them within their shells just as the adult birds
are rendered motionless by the noises.

Fear operates not only between predators and prey but also within the same
species. An alpha male wolf maintains his dominance largely by his ability to instill

fear in would-be usurpers within his group. In mating behavior, especially, males able to intimidate their competitors have a distinct edge in passing on their genes.

Among animals in the wild, the relentless search for food or competition for mates sometimes leads to combat. Usually, though, violence is a last resort. A threatened animal will fight only in a last-ditch effort to live when confrontation is unavoidable. Within species, rivalries may entail aggressive behavior, but often of a highly ritualized sort, a complex ballet of dominance and submission, an intricate interplay of posturing, grunts, and a host of other signals that may seem mysterious to humans but are clearly understood by the animals. The aim of the ritual is to avoid aggression by settling disputes below its threshold. In the end, nature's chief concern is survival; peace is healthier.

In humans, aggression is frequently associated with anger or hatred, or both—emotions difficult (but not impossible) to impute to other animals. The hunter doesn't hate the hunted; predators merely kill in order to live. Similarly, the ritual combat between male stags or dogs seeking mates seldom involves anything so subtle as specifically directed ill will, although in some animals, frustration—being thwarted in an effort to reach a goal—leads to behavior that might convey to the observer a spiteful fury.

Aggressiveness and anger are less primal than fear; for most animals, the combative emotions are subject to more control. Aggression is generally relegated to activities that are most directly concerned with surviving and with passing on an individual's genes and thus perpetuating the species: hunting and mating. Animals usually don't fight out of greed, enmity, or envy.

There are, however, exceptions, found mostly among the evolutionary latecomers, the animals we generally think of and refer to as more "intelligent." Chimpanzee troops have been observed to raid rival groups, to kill others of their own kind. And of course, humans engage in this behavior, in the horrific and time-honored activities of mayhem, murder, and war.

ANNE INNIS DAGG, *University of Waterloo, Ontario, Canada*

Graceful Aggression

Among giraffes, "necking" takes place only between males. This graceful, but aggressive, slow motion fencing match may be one of the ways in which dominance is decided.

Having studied wild giraffes for a year on a ranch near the Kruger National Park in northeast South Africa, I can report that they seem to live largely placid and unemotional lives. However, an exception is expressed in a practice called necking that was common among the males that made up some 70 percent of the herds that I was observing.

In a necking encounter, two males approach each other and stand side by side, sometimes facing the same way, sometimes in opposite directions. One may aim a soft blow with his horns at the other's neck; the other will respond, perhaps by bringing his own head down so that his horns graze his friend's trunk. Often after long pauses they will continue their mellow exchanges, moving their necks in a gentle sparring motion as if practicing in slow motion for a fight. Sometimes one will miss the other entirely with his graceful swing. Sometimes they circle slowly about while exchanging their unpunishing blows.

I never saw necking lead to a real fight between adult bulls, although bouts do occur, perhaps to determine which male is dominant. In such a contest, the bulls hit each other with their horns so solidly that the thwack of combat is audible a hundred meters away. The fight ends with one giraffe running away or being injured, leaving the other victorious.

True fights always involve two males, but the gentler necking behavior is not necessarily restricted to pairs. Occasionally three males will neck, aiming their swings at one another as the spirit moves them. One of them might be a young calf whom an adult will lean over gently. Females in the area may glance at them, but otherwise they pay little attention.

After a few minutes, the participants may lose interest in necking and wander off together to browse. Or necking may alternatively lead to sexual behavior, with one giraffe rubbing his neck along that of his partner and then mounting him briefly.

It is unusual in most species for males to interact so familiarly. Was it because there were so many males in the population? In the Nairobi National Park, where there were slightly more females than males, necking was rarely seen. Yet the males at Fleur de Lys Ranch necked even though females were nearby. Could the behavior be a sociosexual type of bonding between the animals?

Toni Frohoff | *TerraMar Research, Seattle*

The Dolphin's Smile

The bottlenose dolphin on the right exhibits an open-mouth display that human swimmers might regard as "playful." It usually isn't. The open mouth often signals stress and is sometimes a warning.

A friend and I are in the water when a dolphin glides past, a wild glimmer in his eye. Because of the signal's human connotation (not to mention my own ego), I presume that his eye "twinkled" at me because I amuse him and he finds me simply delightful. Then I remember the dolphin trainer's warning that a glimmering eye in this particular dolphin indicates that he's frustrated or stressed and will likely become aggressive. I decide to play it safe and leave the water. My human companion ignores the words of wisdom—and shortly finds himself climbing the twelve-foot-high chain-link fence that surrounds the captive dolphin's enclosure. There he hangs like a wet cat, while the dolphin nips at his feet like a mad shark.

Fortunately, my friend could laugh about this encounter later, because he escaped uninjured. In jest, he reinterpreted the "twinkling" that signaled the attack as the dolphin's "evil eye." But we'd both learned a lesson: Dolphins may be highly skilled at picking up emotional cues from other dolphins, but we humans are not. For us, their anger, frustration, and distress can go unheeded—or be misunderstood.

During years of studying dolphins since this incident, I've witnessed many examples of this interspecies communication problem, particularly during petting, feeding, and swimming programs at dolphinaria. I've often seen captive dolphins exhibiting what I read as clear and blatant indications of aggression or stress while interacting with visitors. Usually the signals are misinterpreted or ignored. The visitors might laugh in response, believing the dolphins are being silly or playful, and go right on with their annoying behavior—teasing them with a fish, perhaps. When the humans find themselves being bitten, or hit by a powerful tail, they're shocked and surprised (and possibly in pain). They're disappointed in the dolphins. It's been my experience, though, that when dolphins are aggressive toward us, it's usually because we've misunderstood them.

People seem to identify with other animals because of the emotions they appear to convey. Dolphins are considered friendly and happy because their mouths form a perpetual "smile," and this is part of what makes them so attractive and endearing. However, the smile is a primate expression, imposed on dolphins by our own primate perceptions. In fact, dolphins don't have the facial muscles to smile—or to frown, for that matter.

Dolphins are also viewed fondly because they're believed to behave altruistically toward people, to save drowning swimmers or lead lost ships to shore. I've actually witnessed a small group of wild spotted dolphins we were swimming with leave us to help another member of

our group, who, unbeknownst to us, had become seriously fatigued and was having trouble swimming back to the boat. On the other hand, I was once "abandoned" by a different group of wild dolphins and found myself in the water with a twelve-foot bull shark instead!

I don't believe that either instance negates the other, or that they prove dolphins are consistently kindly or selfish. What the stories do indicate is that the emotional life of dolphins is probably as multifaceted and colorful as our own, and our appreciation of them needs to encompass their full range of emotional expres-sion—not just the parts we find attractive.

Do we misunderstand dolphins simply because we're unfamiliar with their unique species, their specific behaviors and needs? Possibly, but I also believe we're blinded to their emotional depth by our preconceived ideas of what they are—and what we want them to be.

Douglas Mock | *University of Oklahoma*

Hungry to Survive

Despite having spent nearly thirty years studying egrets and herons—twenty-one of them focusing on the remarkable process of fatal sibling competition ("siblicide"), I must confess near-perfect ignorance of what emotions my subjects experience. This is not the mere knee-jerk denial of one trained to resist all anthropocentrism, but a simple statement of personal absence of knowledge, fitted with the loophole of "near-perfect" that betrays my lingering hunches. Certainly, I can own up to having some ideas on what the birds' mental processes might be; the thousands of hours spent watching nestlings peck, hammer, and stab one another have generated plenty of impressions along the lines of "Owwww, that had to hurt."

First, a quick description is in order. Young great egrets hatch from pale blue eggs no larger than the medium variety in a typical supermarket but grow to a gawky three feet tall within a couple of months. The metabolism that produces this growth explosion isn't supported by parental love (of which I also know nothing objectively), but by frequent parental regurgitations of tiny fish, wadded together in sticky boluses. A parent flies in from the shallows where it has been harvesting these inch-long fish, the nestlings clamor toward the larger bird, and boluses happen.

These meals are violent, and there are two keys to understanding why. First, there are more diners than dinners. For a variety of good reasons, parents tend to aim high when setting up the family's initial size (these are believed to relate to the parents' own uncertainties about food conditions, the risk of accident to hatchlings, and so forth). Thus the life of nestlings begins in a supply-demand mismatch and, in most broods, something's got to give. Think of it as a lethal game of musical chairs. The second key is that each bolus arrives into the hungry sibs' province in the form of a smallish resource that descends from above, which means that it's like an errant basketball rolling off a rim. Whosoever manages to be in the right spot, beneath the parent as it lowers its food-ticket bill, gets the all-important first chance to seize that bill in a scissors-like grip and receive the bolus directly, gape-to-gape. In the parlance of behavioral ecology, the food is "economically defendable." In the parlance of basketball, it pays to "throw some elbow."

Obviously, an egret chick that can intimidate one or both of its nestmates, causing them just the slightest hesitation when reaching for the parent's bill, naturally harvests a greater share of the food. This is self-reinforcing, of course: Eating more means growing more and winning future fights.

Do subordinate chicks experience "fear"? No matter how you define that word, I have to plead ignorance. But I can assure you that they act very much as if they would prefer to avoid physical abuse! In most broods, there's no big puzzle over which chick is in charge and which is most likely to die. Parents incubate the first-laid egg before the second is even laid a day later, and two to three days earlier than the third egg, so embryonic growth commences unevenly and allows the chick A (from the first egg to hatch) to emerge a day or so before B, which is often two days ahead of C. The sooner one escapes from the calcareous confines of its shell and shifts from a finite diet of yolk to the relative largesse of solid food, the more it can grow and exercise.

In these families, the A chick usually pummels both its nestmates briefly, then retires undefeated, dozing between meals in which it typically eats first. The real action thus revolves around B, which starts most of the fights (directed at C), wins most of them, and eats about as well as A. Chick C walks a fine line between needing to reach for food and needing to minimize physical abuse. About a third of C chicks are dead by the end of the first month, so they have plenty of cause for apprehension.

And they do show all the behavioral signs of fear (mixed with hunger and desperation), especially when a parent lands at the nest laden with food. The C chick may cower on the side farthest from the parent. Sometimes, it rushes to the nest rim and hangs its plucked and clotted head far down over the side (where the nape cannot easily be pecked further). A few even leave the nest entirely and hide in whatever vegetation is available, risking a fatal fall in the process. Are they experiencing fear? In their place I certainly would be afraid, but I can't speak reliably for them.

SARAH T. BOYSEN | *Ohio State University*

The Tooth Monster

These two young chimpanzees appear to be having a sociable chat. Their wide repertoire of facial expressions includes lips puckered in friendliness, stretched wide to bare the teeth in aggression, or drawn back in the grimace of fear.

Some years ago I watched Darrell, a young male chimpanzee I was studying, deal with a strange and frightening trauma: One of his baby teeth was loose. He doubtless felt the looseness, along with some minor pain, and after wiggling the offending tooth around a bit, he set about finding some tool to help him dig it out. The best he could come up with was a small plastic toy alligator, which he gave to his lifelong companion, Kermit. Darrell, mouth agape, sat quietly in front of Kermit, who obligingly applied alligator to tooth, quickly extracting it.

What happened next would have been alarming, had I not seen it so many times before (and since) in my twenty-five years of studying chimps. The tooth dropped to the concrete floor, touching off protracted shrieks of alarm. Darrell had felt pain, stuck his finger into the empty socket, and withdrawn blood. But it was not these disagreeable developments that set him screaming: It was the tooth itself. The expelled tooth was the by-product, the little thing that somehow caused pain and blood.

It seems, from all I've witnessed of young chimps' behavior in this situation, that they regard the tooth as responsible for the converging unpleasantness. Of course, while that's theoretically the case, the tooth itself is not imbued with any animate qualities. Even so, the

chimps respond as though it is. Is there any wonder that for us humans the tooth fairy came along, to put a more positive spin on a normal, natural, but sometimes painful, confusing, and frightening childhood experience? For our chimps, there seems to be a tooth bogeyman, instead. In fact, they act as though the tooth itself is the bogeyman.

Of course chimpanzees do not (as humans have long done) invent folkloric creatures and attendant myths to explain away fearsome natural phenomena. Still, there's little question in my mind that chimps experience fear under many of the same circumstances that humans do—the sort of primal fear that spawns myth and folklore. I've seen evidence of this fear not only in the inexplicable loss of a baby tooth, but in chimps' first outdoor experiences with the wind and in their reaction to fake body parts. All three situations have provoked in young chimps such indices of fear as hair standing on end, rapid retreat, and facial expressions known as fear grimaces, during which the corners of the mouth are pulled back to expose the teeth with accompanying intense contraction of the facial musculature. With these go the inevitable screams, alarm calls of varying intensity, depending on the impetus. Sometimes they're bloodcurdling.

I've worked with a number of very young chimpanzees who, in several cases, were born in

captivity and had never been outdoors. Consequently, when the baby chimps came to our project in Ohio, our normal program of intense socialization with teachers, experimenters, and students included daily play outdoors and walks in pastures and woods. On some days the wind is quite strong, and to chimps who've never experienced it before, it seems to be terrifying.

Their typical response is to freeze in position and pull their arms and legs close to their bodies, turning their backs to the offending gusts. They rapidly seek refuge indoors or in the arms of their caretakers. These responses, together with the reports of vigorous displays by wild chimpanzees during thunderstorms and rain, are very reminiscent of our own early fears of such natural events.

To nature's panoply of frights for young chimps, we scientists sometimes supply additions of our own. On one occasion near Halloween, I bought a rubber hand, complete with bloody stump, and simply left it on the floor in the chimps' play area for them to discover. They clearly interpreted the fake limb as potentially

real and decidedly scary. The four chimps who saw it immediately gave forth deafening screams, pulling away from the hand and huddling together, seeking reassurance from one another. Finally, in a daring move, one young male broke away from the group and courageously attacked the hand, piercing its rubber surface repeatedly with his teeth and ultimately hurling it away.

After several minutes of intense screaming, the attacker approached the presumably "dead" hand, touched it lightly, and quickly withdrew his own hand to smell his fingers. Perhaps a "dead" rubber hand should smell different from a "live" rubber hand. Similarly, both in the wild and in captivity, chimpanzees who discover a dead animal have been observed to use sticks or other tools to investigate, then smell the tools. The process appears to be part of their need—not so different from our own—to probe the fearsome mystery of death.

Roland C. Anderson | *The Seattle Aquarium*

Seeing Red

A colleague of mine stated that she was as sure that octopuses have emotions as she was that we haven't proved it yet. And she may be right. Although emotions in octopuses remain unconfirmed by studies of their endocrine systems or parasympathetic nervous systems, it has been theorized that one way octopuses may show emotions is by changing color.

They can alter the hue of their skin in a flash, going from a pearly transparency to white to a fiery, crimson red in a fraction of a second. They accomplish this by the direct neural control of color cells in the skin called chromatophores. These cells come in a variety of hues, largely reds, pinks, browns, blacks, or grays. In addition, octopuses control cells called iridophores that reflect blue colors, and leucophores, which are white. Thus, they have a considerable palette with which to work.

To be sure, not all their chromatic versatility is expended on emotion. Octopuses change colors in order to match their surroundings for camouflage, to communicate with each other, and to startle prey or predators. But there is anecdotal evidence, at least, that points to the possibility that these animals also use color to signal anger.

The Seattle Aquarium, where I've maintained and watched octopuses for twenty-two years, displays the giant Pacific octopus *(Enteroctopus dofleini)*, the largest species in the world.

An octopus "inks," expelling a dark cloud that's useful in distracting predators in the wild. The ink may resemble a phantom octopus, and it may also confuse the predator's senses of taste or smell.

85

(They grow to more than a hundred pounds.) According to a recent survey of public aquariums, this is their most popular and most exhibited species, probably because of its size and its undeserved reputation as a monster.

Giant Pacific octopuses show responses we might construe as anger when their tanks are being cleaned. There are several regular cleaning activities that might well annoy the animals. The glass must be cleaned, wastes and food remains must be removed, drains need to be kept clean, and gravel substrate has to be moved and cleaned. One octopus has a preferred "home" in his tank, directly beneath one of the inflows of new water. He regularly excavates the gravel there and throws shells from the crabs he eats just outside. Unfortunately, the screen over the water drain is also in this spot, and the octopus frequently sits there, covering the drain and causing the tank to overflow. Daily he must be urged elsewhere for the drain to be cleaned and the gravel replaced. The octopus objects to this by wrapping his arms around the gravel-moving tools and long-handled nets and trying to pull them into the water. Moreover, his skin turns a flaming red.

Octopuses in this tank typically weigh between twenty and forty pounds, and they are strong: One forty-pounder managed to escape by moving a sixty-six-pound tank lid. Thus, when our home-loving octopus is nudged aside, a vigorous tug of war ensues. Now an angry red, the creature yanks on the tools, forcing the

cleaner to strip the octopus's arms off them, or even to resort to using an offensive bristly brush to make him move. Sometimes it takes two people to do the routine cleaning: one to clean and one to keep the octopus at bay. The octopus respects and avoids the bristly brush, but still he always turns bright red, angry red, when the tank is cleaned.

It also seems possible that octopuses show anger by squirting well-directed jets of water at whatever displeases them. They breathe by taking water into their mantle and ejecting it out a flexible and directable funnel in a stream that can be used many ways—for swimming; for ejecting ink, wastes, or spermatophores; for digging burrows or digging clams; and for repelling predators. It may even be used in play. Octopuses in shallow water have been seen to blow water jets at floating leaves above them or at fluttering butterflies close to the water's surface, possibly in an effort to remove an annoyance, or possibly just for fun.

Octopuses have proved to have certain personality traits, among them an aggressiveness that might lead to anger if the creature is frustrated. Once I wanted to demonstrate to a visiting BBC videographer what an octopus feels like. I opened the tank, and she stuck her arm in. The octopus immediately turned bright red and tried to pull her hand and arm toward its beak, probably in an attempt to bite her or at least taste her. When she tried to pull her hand back, the octopus threw another suckered arm onto her arm. Each time she peeled one octopus arm off, two more twined around. Eventually she stripped off all the arms and they fell back into the water, whereupon the octopus doused her liberally with a water jet. The bright red octopus quickly directed two more water jets out of its tank before I could close the lid. I think it was angry.

The Seattle Aquarium has twenty-four-hour staffing to handle animal or systems emergencies and to perform routine checks and maintenance. One of our night biologists felt she was being discriminated against by one octopus, since every time she walked by the giant Pacific octopus display tank, the animal would shoot jets of water out at her. Although the tank was tightly sealed, there was a space around the water inlet where water would gush out and drench the woman. She was the only one favored with this peculiar attention. It turned out that she was checking the water inflow with her flashlight, presumably disturbing the octopus, which evidently got angry and retaliated by soaking her.

Octopuses may indeed wear their hearts on their skin—or in their squirts—but it's going to be hard to prove that empirically. Even so, I firmly believe that on many occasions I have witnessed these animals displaying an emotion akin to human anger.

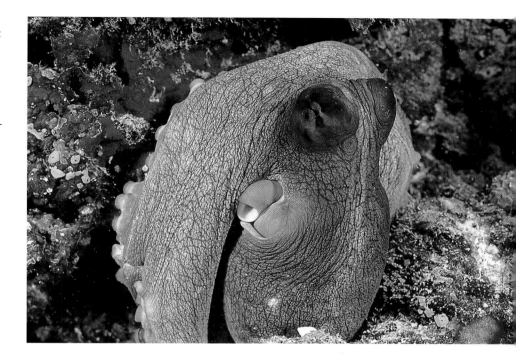

FRANS X. PLOOIJ | *International Research Institute on Infant Studies, Netherlands*

A Slap in the Face

In the Gombe National Park in Tanzania, East Africa, we observers were not allowed to interact with the chimpanzees. If they initiated an interaction, we were supposed to act like pillars of salt. The idea behind this was that the interaction would be no fun and the chimpanzee would stop and not return.

One day, toward the end of my study, I was put to the test. For over a year I'd been observing baby Prof and his mother, Passion. Prof's older sister Pom still lived with her mother and was always around. On this day, Pom became too familiar with me. She came up to me and started grooming my hair. Her gentle touch was wonderful, and it was very tempting to engage in a mutual grooming session. But, according to the rules, I ignored her and acted like the prescribed salt pillar. It didn't work; Pom went on grooming. So I racked my brains for another way to stop her. All of a sudden I remembered how her mother, Passion, had gotten rid of Flint a year earlier.

Flo's son Flint was being a pest. He kept touching baby Prof and refused to stop. Passion couldn't simply tell him off because Flint's mother was highest in the female hierarchy. With Prof clutched to her chest, poor Passion turned her back to Flint to shield the baby from his probing fingers, but all day Flint continued his harassment. Then, at the end of the day, Passion suddenly got up and peered intently across the valley. Flint did, too, and after a while he walked in that direction to have a closer look. As soon as he was out of sight, Passion ran in the other direction with her baby and escaped from Flint.

I decided to try the Passion method. Suddenly, I acted as if I saw something in the distance. In doing so, I moved my head a little from one side to the other, just as owls do. Pom stopped grooming and looked as well, then made a few steps in the direction of my glance and looked back at me. I continued my act, and she walked in the pointed direction and disappeared. I didn't escape as Passion had, but I did resume my observations of Prof.

A little later Pom returned, came straight up to me, and slapped my head, thereafter ignoring me for the rest of the day. The slap was probably a punishment after she realized that I'd deceived her.

Pom fell for the old "Look! What's that?" trick, but she didn't like being fooled—at all. Here, she appears to be pondering weighty matters.

COLIN ALLEN | *Texas A&M University*

Where Pigs and People Fear to Tread

Go to lift thirty kilograms of young pig, and you know fear—and not just your own! At thirty kilograms, pigs no longer have to worry about their mothers rolling on top of them and crushing them to death. Yet they haven't forgotten to squeal as if such a fate is imminent. They start squealing before they're even picked up, and they can squeal loud enough to stand your hair on end. As well they might. Along with having mothers who outweigh them a couple of hundred times, piglets are born with a pair of very sharp teeth that, unless clipped, are used in one of the most ferocious sibling rivalries known among mammals. Thus the ability to make a lot of noise before getting too badly hurt is evidently quite adaptive.

Why was I, a philosophy professor, lifting pigs? It wasn't my idea. Anne Keddy-Hector, a scientist with whom I was collaborating on a cognition study, insisted that we record their weights at the beginning and the end of our work. The only way to do that was to lift the pigs onto the only scale we had available. Beginning weights were easy: six-week-old piglets don't weigh much at all. But weaned piglets practically grow before your eyes, and at twelve weeks some of the faster growers were so large

Pigs are reputed to be among the most intelligent of barnyard animals. They may squeal in anticipation of danger, but they definitely create a chorus when others squeal.

that I was afraid I might put my back out when I tried to lift them.

The dictionary defines fear as an unpleasant emotion caused by anticipation or awareness of danger. Farmers will tell you that pigs are emotional animals. But scientists are more wary. How do we know that pigs experience fear? And how do we know what they anticipate? Scientifically speaking, we don't. Without sufficient data, our intuitive hunches about porcine emotions can be dismissed by skeptics as sheer anthropomorphism. But the exercise of imagining ourselves in the position of the pigs might suggest some way to get the data we need, so let us continue.

When I was ten years old, my two younger sisters and I got stuck in a hotel elevator that kept going up and down from the basement to the top floor and wouldn't stop. My sisters started screaming, but I, trying to be a manly ten-year-old, was determined to maintain a stoic silence. By about the third descent, though, I couldn't help myself. The fear and the screaming were contagious. (Eventually the kitchen staff in the basement of the hotel heard us and got us all out.)

Like human screams, pig squeals certainly create the impression of fear, and they seem to be at least equally contagious. Modern factory-farming techniques place thousands of pigs under one roof. I haven't visited such a facility,

but those who have tell me that one pig squealing can start a chain reaction, and that the resulting noise is so great that many people can't stand to stay in the building. The pigs, of course, don't have the option of getting out.

Diana Bushong, an animal care technician with a soft spot for pigs, once told me that electric fences are ineffective for pigs. If something on the other side makes it worth their while, they learn to run through the fence. But as they run, they start to squeal before they hit it. Banzai pigs! Like us, they appear capable of choosing short-term pain for long-term gain.

There are powerful taboos against thinking of animals that we eat as too much like ourselves, and anecdotes such as these won't convince skeptics who like their bacon served with a clear conscience. Nor should they. What they should do is make us all think harder about how to turn questions about fear and other emotions in other species into scientific investigations of those phenomena.

BARBARA SMUTS | *University of Michigan*

Battle of the Sexes

The complex mating rituals of olive baboons often involve a lengthy series of male advances and female retreats. This male is wearing the "come hither face" meant to reassure a female of his affectionate intentions.

One day while observing wild olive baboons in Kenya, some years ago, I saw a male named Virgil attack a female, Cygne. He was twice her size, and his canines—as long and sharp as a lion's—hovered above her vulnerable neck. After roughing her up for a few minutes, he released her and she ran away to hide in the bushes, still screaming. Several minutes later I found her crouched under a shrub. She wasn't badly hurt; I couldn't see any blood. But she was shaking all over and gasping. Another twenty minutes passed before she calmed down enough to rejoin the troop, and she stayed far away from Virgil the rest of the day.

During a two-year study of Cygne's troop, I saw dozens of attacks like this. I found that pregnant or nursing females endured an average of one male attack each week. Usually the female wasn't bitten, but about one out of every fifty attacks drew blood. This meant that on average, each female was injured by a male about once a year. Males attacked females for many reasons, but some attacks occurred out of the blue, presumably making them even scarier.

Female baboons remain in the group they're born into, but as adolescents or young adults, males leave home to join another troop. Females are most afraid of these strange males. They usually run away whenever one draws near, making it tough for a newcomer to cultivate the bonds with females that are critical to

93

his social and sexual success. Somehow, he must find a way to reassure frightened females.

Crucial first step: Stare at a particular female from a great distance, hoping to make eye contact with her. When she glances your way, flatten your ears against your skull, narrow your eyes, and pull in your chin while shaking your head and shoulders to draw attention to your enchanting expression (called the "come-hither" face). She'll probably ignore you, turn her back, or walk away.

Undaunted, a patient male will continue to make the come-hither face from afar for days, even weeks, while gradually edging closer. Alas, just when he seems to be making headway, she'll scream at him, stomp off, or both. Some males feel so frustrated by such treatment that they succumb to the impulse to run after her. Big mistake. Pursuit can so spook a female that the male is right back to square one. I well remember Ian, a dark-haired male with intense eyes, who repeated this impatient mistake so many times I began to doubt his intelligence.

Some males, however, are endowed with extraordinary sensitivity and rectitude. Sherlock, more than any other male, seemed attuned to the subtle body language that reveals a female baboon's emotional state. When he was courting Justine, if she glanced at him quickly twice in a row, he'd pause, grab a handful of leaves, and eat with great concentration. If she leaned slightly away from him, he'd take a step backward, sit down, and gaze around nonchalantly. If she caught his eye and didn't look away, he would flash a mild come-hither face and grunt softly (another friendly signal). Even then, Sherlock wouldn't try to touch her. Instead,

after a little while he'd saunter off, patiently awaiting the day when Justine would make the come-hither face back at him, a sure sign of willingness to be approached and touched. I could almost hear him whispering, "Don't worry, I just want to be near you for a while. I'm a nice guy. See you later."

Sherlock and Ian—the skilled lover and the hopeless klutz—attempted to join the Eburru Cliffs troop around the same time. A year later, most of the females were still running away from Ian, and he wisely left to try his luck elsewhere. Sherlock, on the other hand, had developed close friendships with six females, more than any other male in the troop, even the old-timers. Male baboons typically stop courting females when they're sixteen to eighteen years old (if they live that long). To my astonishment, when I returned to the Eburru Cliffs troop thirteen years later, Sherlock was still successfully wooing at the age of twenty-four (about ninety in human years).

Sherlock knew the secrets all animals must learn if they want to earn the trust of someone frightened of them: Carefully observe the other, express your friendly intentions, keep your overtures subtle, and wait for the fearful one to make the first move. I learned the finer points of the art from Sherlock, whose ways I successfully imitated during my efforts to convince 130 frightened baboons to accept my presence.

On returning to the human world, I was sad to discover that many people are more like Ian than Sherlock, lacking intuitive knowledge of how to approach a fearful animal (or child). Perhaps by observing the masters among us, like Sherlock, we could all learn how to help others move from fear to trust.

ANNE RASA | *Bonn University, Germany*

A False Alarm

It was a perfect morning in the Taru Desert. The sun was just clearing the treetops, and a gentle breeze rustled the dry grass. I sat in the Land Cruiser, watching one of my dwarf mongoose groups moving slowly along, trailing its little flock of grasshopper-hunting hornbills behind it like a banner. Blackie, one of the subordinate mongoose males, was on guard duty in a nearby Commiphora tree, and the fluttering hornbills clearly marked the direction in which the group was foraging. Everything was peaceful, and I poured myself a cup of tea from my thermos and settled back to enjoy the nicest part of the day.

Suddenly there came a loud, explosive snort from somewhere near my right elbow. My tea ended in my lap, the hornbills shot vertically into the trees, Blackie took a flying leap from his guard post, and the mongooses galloped to the nearest termite mound, diving instantly into its ventilation shafts. Total panic! I very slowly turned my head and peered sideways out the car window. Standing near my back bumper was a beautiful Peter's gazelle buck, his dark eyes staring, ears pricked forward, and nostrils quivering, his attention riveted on something in front of me. His warning snort had totally destroyed the morning's quiet, and I carefully searched the area in front of the car with my binoculars to discover which predator was approaching. Nothing.

The hornbills, all sleek-feathered and nervous, were peering around from their perches; the mongooses were playing it safe and keeping underground. The area around me was still as a grave. Then I heard a gentle rustling in the grass, and the little buck, still pressed close to the Land Cruiser, moved forward until his nose was about level with the car's side mirror. I could have reached out and touched him. Another explosive, sneeze-like snort, and the buck whirled and ran to hide behind my back bumper again. I still couldn't see what could have frightened him so badly.

The hornbills, getting more and more agitated, started a slow *wok-wok-wok* alarm call of their own and flew off, one by one. A mongoose stuck its head out of the termite mound, looked around briefly, screamed a warning, and shot back in again. Still not an enemy in sight.

It was only after the whole scenario had repeated itself a second and third time that it finally dawned on me what was happening. Because I was downwind of him, the gazelle caught my scent only when he reached the level of my side mirror, and this set off his alarm snort and panicky flight. He was obviously not connecting "car" with "human scent" and was hiding safely behind the bulk of the Land Cruiser from the human enemy he could clearly smell but not see somewhere in front of him.

The yellow hornbill and the Peter's gazelle are both part of an elaborate alarm system in the wilds of Kenya. An animal sensing danger can transmit its distress to many other species.

I had visions of this little pantomime continuing for hours as the buck slowly moved forward once more, passing less than a foot from me before snorting, whirling, and running for the shelter of the back bumper once more. Startled mongoose heads popped out of the mound, looked all around and, to a chorus of warning calls, popped back in again. So much for observation of a quiet morning's foraging. As the little buck started forward for the fifth time, I slowly stretched my arm out of the window and made shooing motions with my hand right in front of his nose. He whirled and with two tremendous leaps disappeared into the trees. I was left staring at an empty termite mound with not a hornbill in sight. It took much longer than usual—more than half an hour—for the first mongoose guard to come out, hair on end, peering around for the invisible source of danger and warning softly. It was another two hours before things got back to normal, the mongoose group with its hornbill retinue slowly setting off again on its interrupted foraging tour.

This episode taught me two lessons. It really brought home how closely the animals in Kenya's harsh Taru Desert depended on one another. The danger that one animal sensed was instantly transmitted through its alarm call to all the others in the area, whether they were the same species or not, and everyone fled. The funny thing was that for the gazelle, I was the source of danger, but over the weeks the car and I had become such a harmless and constant part of the mongooses' lives that they practically ignored me. The mongooses themselves taught me the second lesson by taking so long to venture out from the safety of the mound. They weren't able to spot the "predator" that the buck told them was there, and since they didn't connect me with danger any more, they'd fallen back on one of survival's basic tenets— "Beware the dragon that you can't see"—and had been especially wary of emerging again with an "invisible predator" around.

BERND HEINRICH | *University of Vermont*

Hopping Mad

Like other emotions, anger is a feeling that wells up inside us, in this case a displeasure generally directed at another sentient being, or beings, who can at least potentially respond. In us, anger is aroused by myriad things, small and large—a thoughtless driver who cuts us off in traffic, a thief who tries to pick our pocket, a loved one who disappoints us in some significant way. (In us, anger can also be aroused by memory, by re-creating anger-inducing events in our mind.)

Anger is not confined to humans. I've seen different individual ravens express anger in different contexts. I saw one get angry at me when I blocked his way. I've often seen ravens get angry with another bird who raided a cache or took away a piece of food. But the most intense anger I've witnessed in birds came when I climbed to a nest to take young. In this case, the anger was expressed in a progression of protests, beginning with high-pitched repetitive alarm calls. At this stage, the emotions of heightened alertness and anger were not yet clearly defined. But as I got closer to the nest, the calls became long and rasping, and finally the parent birds were hopping up and down on branches near me, their feathers fluffed out, emitting vocalizations resembling snarls and growls. At that point I began to sense that anger could indeed be an

Male and female ravens form pairs, preening each other's feathers and hunting together. In some cases, one bird will distract a predator so the other can steal its prey, which they then share.

effective threat. Finally, as I handled one of the young and it yelled in protest, the parents swooped over my head, landed on the closest branches, uttered rasping growls, ripped off twigs and flung them aside, then hammered on their perches with all their might.

Anger has adaptive value—survival value in the ultimate evolutionary sense. Animals exhibit anger to warn potential adversaries of what cannot or will not be tolerated. Thus, anger sets up boundaries or limits. Some of the more intelligent animals, us included, can express anger consciously, with awareness of its nature and its effects. In such cases, anger becomes even more effective because it can be modified or manipulated—faked, suppressed, heightened, or redirected—to suit specific purposes. We, and presumably certain other animals, not only feel anger but are able to analyze it, to modulate it rationally.

The anger that I've seen in ravens, however, was likely pure and primal. It did not (at least to me) seem tempered with rationality, although being a skeptical scientist I can't be sure. There's no reason to assume the ravens' expression of anger was influenced by conscious attempts to "drive the predator off." They simply felt and exhibited anger—likely tempered by fear. Some shier birds depart on seeing a human near their nest. Bolder ones protest vigorously, but from a safe distance in

the air. They seem to understand that they can't do much against a human intruder, just as we express little anger at a hurricane because we cannot influence it. Fear or caution are more appropriate reactions, and we hide from the oncoming storm. The ravens react similarly; their responses are geared to the object, and to the fact that it's a being who will understand and hence respond.

Fear, anger, love, hate, and curiosity are emotions that illuminate much of raven behav-

ior in terms of human understanding of it. Without invoking emotions we are left to explain the birds' behavior by resorting to complex rationality theories or to the cliché of stimulus and response. I exclude neither rationality nor stimulus and response as an explanation of ravens' "emotional" behavior. They are probably parts of the answer. They are just not the central issue.

Meerkats can be fierce out of all proportion to their two-pound size. The upright "flagged" tail position shown here is typical in confrontations.

DAVID MACDONALD | *Oxford University and Cornell University*

Desert Warfare

Under the blazing sun of the Kalahari Desert in the 1980s, there lived a group of meerkats called the Kwang Raiders. Its members were Scar Shoulder, the patriarch; his second lieutenant, named Scar Chest; and two young males known by the undignified but apt names of Smallballs and his younger brother Nanoballs. Probably they were both Scar Shoulder's sons, but Scar Chest had worked tirelessly to help raise them. These four males clustered around the two females, Pinthroat and Perfect. Romance was in the air, and the bond that had for years united Scar Shoulder and Scar Chest grew strained, then snapped.

Just after noon one November day, I spotted five Raiders pounding in pursuit of a lone meerkat. Far ahead, their fleeing victim wove a trail through the bushes. When the Raiders paused, Smallballs detached himself from the band and ran on in solitary vendetta. When at last he returned, the Raiders writhed in a congratulatory hubbub of antagonism. Far away, the lone meerkat huddled on the dune. It was Scar Chest, set upon by the very companions for whom he'd toiled as helper and guard.

That night, Scar Chest crossed the border into the territory of the Woodlanders, the Raiders' long-standing territorial enemies—for the first of several times. This was the start of a remarkable few days.

The Raiders' vendetta against him left Scar Chest torn and bloody, exposed and alone in the desert. His wounds suppurated, but he survived. Then, as unexpectedly as they'd begun, the Raiders' attacks on him ceased, and he was back among them, once again the stalwart guard. Now he seemed intent on persuading them to follow him. Three days after his return to the fold, his frustration bubbled over. As soon as the Raiders awoke, Scar Chest began to stare to the north. He ran ahead, the mob followed; they paused, he ran back to them and then led off again. Bit by bit they followed him north. They had scarcely time to forage before he led them on. At last, even the meerkats' central tenet of keeping together couldn't stand his pace. The next morning he drew three hundred meters ahead of them, and they let him go.

Following Scar Chest's path, the group edged ever closer to the Woodlanders' border. Then, in the far distance, their trailblazer came into sight. More than a hundred meters ahead, Scar Chest was running toward them, and hard on his heels came the Woodlanders.

The two mobs were perfectly matched, five to five, and gang war flared instantly. The teams faced each other, all tails flagged, legs stiff. They began to bound, rocking higher and higher. All, that is, except Scar Chest. He was in slinky mode. Tail down, body low, he scuttled between the warring groups like a sheepdog seeking the moment to turn his flock. The teams charged. The Raiders won the advantage; the Woodlanders regrouped and counterattacked. For an hour I watched from the sidelines, thunderstruck at the ferocity of their war. A noise distracted me: At my feet Scar Chest was sitting, also watching the action.

The two factions then drifted apart, the heat draining from their combat. But Scar Chest, now back with the Raiders, broke away and ran toward the Woodlanders. Thirty meters from them he stopped. They started violently, but did nothing. He ran to ten meters, seeming to flaunt himself. They charged. Scar Chest raced back to the Raiders who, seeing the Woodlanders bearing down, charged, too.

Running to and fro, Scar Chest's interventions seemed to escalate and prolong the war. But at midmorning, Scar Shoulder and the Raider females turned and ran. Scar Chest was dashing back and forth between the two younger Raiders, Smallballs and Nanoballs, and in the confusion the next thing I saw was the three of them skirting the Woodlanders, hugging the ground as they closed in surreptitiously. Now the game was kidnap.

The three Raider males, sometimes together, sometimes in turn, tried to reach the Woodlander females. The junior Woodlander male had fled; the senior one flung himself at the Raider males, as did his three females. But while he chased one Raider, the other two males moved in. Slowly the Woodlanders were pushed into retreat, backward up the steep sand dune. Before they reached the top, their male had attacked another dozen times, but he was fading. They crossed the dune crest, and it was over. The senior Woodland male was in terrified flight, the three kidnappers bunched close behind him and the three Woodland females racing behind, seemingly trying to defend their male. We lost sight of them.

Meanwhile, Scar Shoulder, Pinthroat, and Perfect were attacking the Woodlanders' junior male, who appeared to be trying to join them. Later, we found two of the kidnappers on a sandy plateau in the dunes, herding their reluctant female conquests. But Smallballs had gone.

The mood was frantic. The three female Woodlanders were manifestly outraged by the kidnap. Over and over they yelped the bark of lost meerkats, as they stared at the forlorn and distant figure of their deposed mate. They tried to break away, but Scar Chest and Nanoballs headed them off. The victors could scarcely concentrate on their task, however; they were beside themselves with excitement. They scent marked again and again, twining their tails together, reversing into each other and rubbing their bottoms together. They marked each other, and the vegetation and the females, and for the first time I saw Scar Chest repeatedly mark the burrow entrances, which is the prerogative of a dominant male.

And so the day passed in punitive chases of the forlorn deposed male, in shepherding the unwilling females, and in orgiastic scent marking. By midafternoon, Smallballs was back, and the three males lurched around, tails entwined in hours of self-congratulation. By nightfall, though one female still yelped to her lost mate, the others were beginning to groom with their new companions. The following day, there was a prolonged counterattack from the ousted males, but the three kidnappers successfully repelled it. The celebrations lasted for five days. Scar Chest was the first to calm down, adopting a new and rather stately detachment, while Smallballs stood guard, and the youthful Nano let success go to his head, frenziedly smearing his scent over everything he could find, including my feet.

And so it was that Scar Chest came to rule the Woodlanders. Did he, as it seemed, plan the clash and kidnapping? Who can say, but in years to come he was to father many young and fight many battles.

ANNE INNIS DAGG | *University of Waterloo, Ontario*

A Furious Complaint

Camels often seem to have a sarcastic sneer on their faces, but this doesn't indicate hostility. Instead, look out for the ones with their ears folded back against their heads—they're in a bad mood.

During two summers I accompanied Hilde Gauthier-Pilters, a world authority on camels, into the Sahara Desert on camel safaris. She was researching camel physiology under conditions of extreme heat, calculating the amount of water each consumed at wells and through browsing, and how much they excreted. I was filming their gaits, which I planned to analyze when I returned home to Canada.

On these trips, during which we lived intimately with the camels, I remember most poignantly their twice-daily rage. Their angry bellows overwhelmed our campsites each time the camelmen forced them to rise to their feet after they'd been loaded so that we could continue our trek through the desert.

Shortly after sunrise, and after our long midday break, the two Mauritanian men would round up the four camels who'd been browsing on any sparse vegetation they could find. Because they'd been hobbled (one leg tied up with a rope so they could only stagger along on three legs), they hadn't gone far. Either the men tracked them in the sand, or they spotted Hilde and me standing by the heads of two of them, counting the number of mouthfuls of leaves or grass they were eating.

The men led the camels to our campsite on the sand, commanded them to lie down, and then loaded them with bulky saddles; dunnage bags stuffed with food, clothing, and bedding; and water, always water, contained in goatskins suspended from ropes.

When everything was fastened in place, the men ordered the animals to rise. Then, the camels' anger at their hard lives welled up into great waves of fury that rolled across the desert, filling Hilde and me with guilt and distress. The animals struggled to raise their hindquarters first, the baggage shifting forward as they did so, and when that was accomplished they strained to straighten their front legs, too, calling out angrily all the while. Their loads weren't horrendous—about a hundred kilos, or 220 pounds, when the record for weight carried by a camel is three times that much for a short distance—but they were heavy enough. To keep the weight down, we almost always walked rather than rode.

When the camels were standing and still complaining lustily, the men fastened further bits and pieces onto them—a bucket to pull water from the wells, a kettle, cooking oil, pots, lamps, ropes, an ax, and a rifle.

The heat of each July day was devastating to us and surely oppressive to the camels, too, although by the time we set off they'd stopped their loud complaints. They plodded steadily forward for many hours each day, tied loosely head to tail, marching endlessly across the sand or gravel. We walked beside them in our turbans and baggy clothes, conscious of every breath we took, the hot wind searing our lungs.

Sometimes for Hilde's research we collected their urine in tin cups so that we could measure its volume, but often we let the trickle of liquid blow against our bare legs to cool them.

We could drink during the day if we wished, stopping a camel so that we could slurp up water tasting of tar from the goatskin neck hole. But the camels weren't so lucky. It was heavy work pulling a bucket of water from a fifty-foot-deep well, and thirsty camels could have drunk dozens of buckets each. Unless their ribs were showing to indicate that they were thoroughly dehydrated, however, they had to go without. Once we met a lost camel at a well, but the men refused to pull water for it; if it weren't thirsty, it would wander off into the desert and its owner would never find it, they told us. Of course, if it didn't get water soon it would die, but they didn't say that.

Many desert travelers scorn the camel, objecting to the noise it makes and to the superior expression on its face. Perhaps it annoys them that camels seem so independent and aloof, declining to have their noses or necks stroked in the way that horses seem to enjoy. But then life for a camel is unbelievably hard. No wonder they're impervious to friendly approaches from humans. No wonder they protest the outrage each day of being hungry and thirsty and laden with heavy packs they must carry for long hours.

105

RONALD J. SCHUSTERMAN | *University of California, Santa Cruz*

Pitching a Fit

LEFT: *Rio tosses her duck decoy in frustration at making a mistake.*

RIGHT: *Rio and decoy in a calmer moment*

Even when captive animals are some distance away from visitors or caretakers, they're quite capable of expressing their anger, peevishness, or resentment at them. This can be done in a variety of ways, depending on the species and environmental circumstances, and it can include hurling or throwing whatever is handy, spitting water or partially (or even fully) digested food, or splashing water at the intended targets (which have sometimes included me).

I've observed such events many times in my career, and the animals I'm most familiar with who engage in such mischief are bottlenose dolphins, harbor seals, California sea lions, and common chimpanzees. In the late 1960s, I was being shown some female harbor seals who were kept in a pool located in a small house. My host, Michael Biggs, told me to be careful as we opened the door because I could get soaking wet. Sure enough, as we tried to enter the laboratory, one of the harbor seals began splashing torrents of water over the sides of the pool, spraying it so far that all we could do was duck and flee before we got drenched. My understanding from Michael was that he had to endure this every time he made his observations and took blood samples from his animals. In other words, his animals would allow their blood to be drawn, but only if they could soak him down first.

One of my most vivid memories of hurling behavior as an aggressive act was one that took place at Kewalo Basin in Hawaii during research on teaching dolphins an artificial language. The female dolphin Ake had just been given a series of gestural signals by a young intern. The cues were produced at the side of the pool, and when Ake didn't respond correctly, she was given negative feedback. A moment later, the dolphin grabbed a large plastic pipe floating on the water's surface and flung it unerringly at the poor, unsuspecting intern. The pipe missed the young lady's head by inches, and all the students, volunteers, and researchers around the pool gasped.

Very similar incidents have occurred with California sea lions who were being given visual instructions in both artificial language and matching-to-sample, a task requiring an animal to fetch an object identical to one being displayed. In each case an object was flung at the signaler following negative feedback because the complete task had not been correctly carried out by the sea lion. For example, Rio, one of our sea lions at Long Marine Lab, was given an instruction to retrieve the objects in a pool following an incorrect response in a matching-to-sample task. She retrieved one of the objects, a duck decoy painted black, but instead of carrying it to the side of the pool and placing it at

106

the signaler's feet, as she'd been trained to do, she grabbed the duck decoy's head in her mouth and hurled the heavy object directly at the signaler. This behavior occurred many times with an assortment of objects and always followed an incorrect response.

The clearest example I ever saw of an animal getting revenge on one of its caretakers goes back to my pre- and post-doctoral days at the Yerkes Laboratory of Primate Biology in Orange Park, Florida. It was a cold, misty December morning, and I'd noticed my friend and colleague Larry Sharp standing in front of a young male chimpanzee, Franz, who was in one of the large end cages in a row of cages. Franz, one of several common chimpanzees at Yerkes, was known to be a feces thrower; that is, he would scoop up excrement and throw it underhand as he charged his intended victim.

The fecal material usually would hit the cage wire and shatter like a shotgun blast.

Larry had been one of Franz's favorite targets, but that morning Larry noticed that the fecal material had been cleaned up and there was none available for Franz to throw. Consequently, he went to the front of the cage and began teasing Franz, saying, "You've got no fecal material today, and you can't get me—na na na na naaaa-na!" Franz was hanging on the fence, weaving back and forth, staring at Larry throughout the taunting. When Larry finished, Franz regurgitated partially digested cookies that he had been fed only a few minutes earlier. The awful-smelling stuff sprayed all over Larry, and Franz started running around the cage as if doing a victory dance. He'd gotten his revenge on Larry Sharp.

107

IRENE PEPPERBERG | *University of Arizona*

Ruffled Feathers

My career has been spent demonstrating that Grey parrots *(Psittacus erithacus)* aren't mindless mimics but creatures capable of communicating information beyond what's involved in their immediate emotional states. My primary concern is cognition—the birds' thought processes, which can be tested objectively and quantified. Nevertheless, I find rare situations where emotionality must be considered as a possible factor that affects how birds think.

A case in point involves an experiment that was designed as part of a study on what we call object permanence. We test whether the parrots have a "mental picture" of an item we've hidden from them by examining whether they react when they find an actual object that is different from their possible mental picture. We trick the birds, showing and then hiding a favorite treat, and then surreptitiously substituting something of little interest.

Confronted with the "wrong" thing, parrots react with what a nonscientist would characterize as "surprise" and "anger." After removing the cover of a box and finding a food pellet rather than the expected cashew, one bird, Alex, turned away from the apparatus and toward us. He narrowed his eyes, puffed his feathers, opened his wings slightly, and lowered his head—signs that we've come to interpret as anger, or at least a clear threat: The slit-eyed look is usually a prelude to our being bitten if we persist in the offending behavior. In a later trial he extended his repertoire, banging his beak rapidly on the table—another sign of frustration or displeasure.

I can't say for certain, of course, what Alex might have been feeling, or how his emotions, if any, might have influenced his thinking. It does appear, however, that Alex had certain expectations. And when those expectations weren't met, he let us know it.

Highly intelligent Grey parrots, such as Alex, are able not only to speak but, it seems, with proper training, to understand at least some of what they say. Alex asks for one of his preferred treats—pasta— by name. He likes it raw.

RUUD VAN DEN BOS | *Utrecht University Animal Welfare Centre, Netherlands*

Cantankerous Cats

Imagine the following scene with Jim Davis's cartoon cat, Garfield: Garfield sits next to his food bowl, chewing his abundantly present food. Enter Darlene, his lady friend. She leans expectantly toward the bowl. Garfield growls at her. "I thought you asked me for dinner," says the miffed Darlene. "Old habits are difficult to get rid of," sighs Garfield.

Now imagine the following actual scenes involving real cats:

Scene 1: Lisa sees Diane drinking water from a small fountain. Diane notices Lisa and runs to a hiding place, chased by Lisa.

Scene 2: Karen sits on a platform. Lisa jumps on a sink just below the platform, startling and threatening Karen. But Karen holds her ground, so Lisa moves from the sink to a shelf above Karen's platform and starts threatening her from there. After a while, Lisa just moves away. This behavior is repeated a number of times that day.

Scenes 1 and 2 are taken from one of the first groups of cats I ever observed in captivity, a group of nonspayed females. What do these scenes reveal about Lisa's emotions prior to, during, or after the conflicts? Is she, for instance, angry while showing aggressive behavior? Or is the aggression prompted by anger—or spite, or sheer menace—and is she sensitive to the emotion that the aggressive behavior inspires in its targets?

Readers familiar with Garfield know the answers, since they obligingly appear in his behavior and in the text balloons over his head: Yes, he's spiteful, a menace, and though he may be sensitive to others' emotions, he generally ignores them. In Real Cats Scene 1, Garfield would simply say, "That's mine! Hands off!" He would be defending a resource (water, in this case). In Scene 2, Garfield might be acting out of spite, in response to some remark about his weight, for instance.

With real cats, we can agree on at least two aspects of Scene 1: There's no resource without conflict, and aggressive behavior can be observed and recorded. And we could ask: How do cats signal their aggression-related moods? Obviously, some vocal and postural expressions come into play: Read my ears (pointed forward or backward), read my posture (high or low), and read my voice (hissing, caterwauling).

But at a more subtle level, signals of aggression are harder to recognize, at least for the human observer. Often one sees a cat moving cautiously close to a second cat—one who's normally more aggressive—without any obvious signs of threat. Does this mean that the first cat is cautious because it expects aggression from the second cat, or that the second cat sends out

This tabby cat shows signs of fear, or anger, or both: ears flattened, mouth opened in a warning hiss, claws beginning to extrude. In addition, his hair is bristling, which makes him look bigger to his possible adversary.

some signals of aggression that we don't recognize? We don't yet have an answer.

Nor can we yet scientifically answer the threshold question: Do animals have emotions? It's a controversial issue in scientific circles. A minimal approach is to say that emotions arising from immediate internal and external signals direct an animal's future behavior in an integrated way that benefits the individual. So, the feeling of pain (from a wound, say) serves to discourage future activities that would slow the healing process. And anger (from seeing another individual taking a valuable resource, say) prompts the threatened animal to act to secure the resource for himself or herself.

The latter proposition could apply both to Garfield and to Lisa in Scene 1. And as both examples show, the apparent anger occurs regardless of whether the resource is abundant or scant. This exaggerated or near-involuntary aspect may be an essential feature of emotions.

Scene 2 is less straightforward in its interpretation; Lisa's behavior is not easily explained in simple terms. Maybe it's a general territorial conflict (protecting a resource) and therefore comparable to Scene 1. Or maybe Lisa had just been harassed by another cat and has decided to take it out on Karen. In this case, the behavior would be driven by the feeling of frustration.

Although Garfield is sensitive to what his behavior inspires in Darlene—she feels offended, he feels guilty—I very much doubt whether real cats would have any such compunctions. From what I've seen over the years, it appears a cat may read another cat's behavior, but not its emotions. So Scenes 1 and 2 are not easily scientifically accessible, but they certainly force one to rethink again and again the question of emotions in animals.

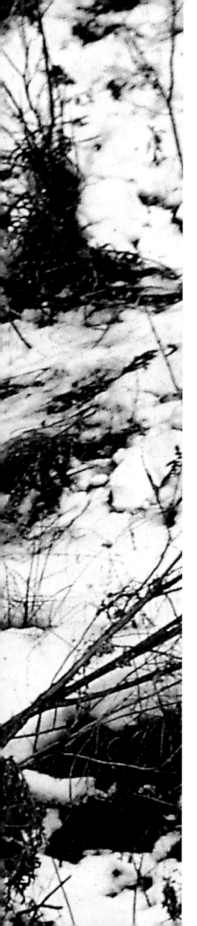

JOY AND GRIEF

When Charles Darwin wrote that animals other than human beings can know both happiness and misery, he was stating the obvious: Among the secondary emotions, none are so abundantly apparent in animals as are joy and grief.

Dogs bark with delight; cats purr with contentment. Rats emit little clicks of pleasure if you tickle them. Dolphins chuckle when making friends. And on it goes. Animals show joy when they groom one another, eat, get free of confinement. In welcoming friends and family, they wax ecstatic. Greeting ceremonies in African wild dogs involve cacophonies of happy whining and squealing, the propeller-like wagging of tails, smiles and nudges, sniffing and licking, abandoned squirming and flailing of legs. Elephant families celebrate reunions with whirls and bellows, rumbling and trumpeting their delight.

Most of all, perhaps, animals express joy in play. I once saw a young elk in Rocky Mountain National Park running across a snow field, jumping and twisting, stopping to catch his breath, then repeating the whole exercise with boundless energy. Similarly, buffaloes have been known to rush onto ice fields and slide, like children on frosty sidewalks, bellowing with the simple fun of it. Running, leaping, wrestling, chasing objects or one another or their own tails, animals at play are the very symbols of the unfettered joy of life.

And they're no less extreme in their sorrow. Like humans, other animals suffer monumentally at separation and loss. The death of an infant, sibling, mate, parent, or friend can cause them untold sadness. Sea lion mothers witnessing attacks on their calves by killer whales wail in anguish. Elephants stand guard over a stillborn baby for days, heads and ears drooping in dejection. Some geese who've lost their mates waste with grief, their eyes sinking into their sockets, their vulnerability making them defenseless against the attacks of other birds.

PRECEDING PAGES:
A young panda slides down a snow-covered slope in Wolong Preserve, China's largest panda sanctuary.

Among social animals, mourning is common and its symptoms clear. Grieving animals may withdraw from their group and seek seclusion, impervious to all attempts by their fellows to draw them out. They may sit in one place, motionless, staring vacantly into space. They stop eating and lose interest in sex. Sometimes they become obsessed with the dead individual. They may try to revive it and, failing that, carry the corpse around until it decomposes.

Some or all of these behaviors have been seen in domestic dogs and cats and in elephants and many nonhuman primates. Occasionally, such animals die of grief.

Behavioral scientists find grief something of a mystery, since it seems to have no adaptive value in an evolutionary sense; that is, it doesn't seem to help an individual survive or reproduce. Perhaps, some theorize, mourning strengthens useful social bonds among survivors. In any case, it must have some function, since it manifestly has evolved among many animals, mammals and beyond. Maybe grief is the price of commitment, that wellspring of both happiness and sorrow.

DENISE L. HERZING | *Florida Atlantic University*

The Pleasure of Their Company

Young dolphins come in many stripes. Some are shy, some bold, some mischievous, some overly cautious about life. But one thing they all share is the pure joy of being a young dolphin in a new and mysterious world. They express their joy in the pure exuberance of swimming faster than a companion, in testing their prowess while riding a boat's bow wave, in tender moments with their mothers, playing with seaweed in the gentle, gin-blue sea.

Spotted dolphins live in the clear waters of the Bahamas; and although it's a challenging place to earn a living, they have here a reliable food source, social stability, and many friends. More than any of their dolphin kin, the spotted dolphins are gregarious, both with other species and with humans who occasionally appear in their environment.

In 1991, Rosemole, a female I'd known since 1985 when I began my long-term work in the Bahamas, had her first offspring, Rosebud. Both mother and daughter were sweet and shy. I've spent considerable time in the water with them, especially when Rosebud was growing up. I remember many hours of drifting along in the ocean, watching them gently play with a piece of sea grass by passing it back and forth, one dragging it down to the bottom and encouraging the other to pick it up. Then, with a gentle roll and stroke, they would reaffirm their physi-

cal bond and begin again. This felt to me like a quietly joyful moment for them both.

When a dolphin leaps out of the water, we often interpret this as joyful play, and sometimes it is. Ironically, though, the leaps occur more often during an aggressive encounter, when one dolphin chases another out of the water. By way of contrast, dolphins seem to extract joy simply from moving slowly in one another's company, drifting along in a gentle current, quietly touching, perhaps exploring together a sponge on the seafloor.

Quiet pleasures aside, dolphins also have their moments of joyful excitement. During the summer of 1999, I was in the water with three rambunctious calves of the year, Blossom, Tyler, and Uni. Racing and darting between me and a drifting boat, without their mothers to discipline them, they seemed to experience joy. I know I was exhilarated just watching them, seeing the pure vitality of the calves, young and free, with fresh eyes for exploring the adventure-filled ocean, for defining and experiencing dolphin joy.

Highly sociable, dolphins not only play together but also hunt and feed as a group. Searching for fish or squid, they travel in a broad formation, scanning for food by means of echolocation, a sort of animal sonar.

KAY E. HOLEKAMP AND LAURA SMALE | *Michigan State University*

A Hostile Homecoming

Two hyenas attack an interloper in their territory. One bites the victim's face while his comrade circles, jaws dribbling blood from a freshly inflicted wound. The intruder survived the attack but was badly mauled.

Spotted hyenas are large African carnivores that live in social groups called clans. Although widely believed to be skulking carrion eaters, spotted hyenas are in fact very efficient hunters who feed mainly on large antelope that they kill themselves. A group of hungry hyenas can reduce a four-hundred-pound antelope to a few scattered bones in less than half an hour. They have such formidable teeth and such enormous bite strength that a single hyena can rip the belly out of an adult wildebeest or crack open a giraffe leg bone two inches in diameter.

When all members of an animal society carry weapons this effective, opponents in intense fights are likely to sustain debilitating physical injuries. Therefore, much of the aggression occurring among members of a hyena clan appears fairly mild and ritualistic. For example, when one hyena is being bothered by one of its clan mates, or when it wants to displace a clan mate from food, it often needs only approach the other animal or wave its head toward that animal in a mild threat. If one hyena fails to heed a low-level threat from another, then aggression may escalate to lunging, snapping, or chasing. However, only the most intense aggressive interactions involve one hyena actually biting another.

During twelve years of observing one large hyena clan in the Talek region of southwest Kenya, we've occasionally seen aggression

119

of extraordinary intensity. In one such case, an adult female hyena named Little Gullwing, or LG, was attempting to rejoin the Talek clan after a yearlong absence. Unfortunately for LG, she had been gone from the Talek clan for so long that she was now no longer perceived by her former clanmates as a member of the group. Instead, she was treated as an interloper in the Talek clan's territory.

In contrast to the relatively mild, ritualized hostility seen so commonly during aggressive interactions between clan mates, aggression directed at intruders is fierce and unrestrained. After all, the territory that is defended by any hyena clan usually supports enough antelope to sustain only the members of that clan, so cooperative defense of the clan's food supply requires the strong discouragement of visitors from neighboring clans.

Now, as we watched LG approach a group of Talek hyenas after her long absence, she stopped hundreds of meters from her former clanmates, flattened her ears back against her head, lowered her tail between her legs, and curled her lips into a grimace-like grin of appeasement. Her fear was almost palpable, but her desire to rejoin her clan was also clearly very strong, so she slowly began walking again toward her former comrades. When she was about fifty meters from them, LG began vigorously bobbing her head up and down and side to side to signal the Talek hyenas that her intentions were strictly peaceful.

At this point the entire group of Talek hyenas started to move together toward LG. As

though of one mind, they all raised and bristled their black-tipped tails, thereby revealing high excitement. Their forward-cocked ears and bristled manes also signaled their hostile intentions. As they drew near her, LG stopped walking, dropped to the ground, folded back her forepaws, and began crawling forward again on her carpals. This carpal-crawling behavior is the most extreme form of appeasement in the hyena behavioral repertoire—a groveling action that often inhibits biting and other forms of intense aggression among clanmates. But it failed to work this time.

One adult Talek female first broke away from the approaching group and rushed toward LG, who froze in her groveling position but continued grinning and wildly bobbing her head. The Talek female stood over LG for an instant and then bit her sharply on the shoulder. LG screamed in pain, and blood immediately welled up in the puncture wounds inflicted by the other female's sharp canine teeth. Now all the other Talek hyenas rushed to surround LG, standing over her, bristling, then biting at all exposed parts of her body. LG screamed again and again, crouching to protect her vulnerable belly and trying frantically to parry the onslaught of bites with her open mouth. One Talek hyena grabbed her ear and backed away from LG, who twisted her head in an effort to escape the pain.

Meanwhile, another Talek hyena grabbed the skin between LG's shoulder blades and shook its head vigorously back and forth while also yanking upward in the same violent motion used to tear meat from an antelope carcass. With so many hyenas tearing at her and draw-

Tail up and bristled and ears cocked forward in a classic aggressive stance, one hyena assaults another. The outclassed opponent cowers, ears flattened and tail between its legs to signal submission.

ing blood at every bite, LG twisted her body sideways in an effort to escape. But this movement exposed her belly, and in an instant another Talek hyena sank its teeth into LG's udder and ripped off one of her two teats, leaving it hanging by only a few strands of tissue. With one final scream of agony, LG finally managed to leap up and race away from the angry mob of Talek animals, which pursued her at top speed until she fled into the territory of a neighboring clan. Having removed her from their territory, the Talek hyenas instantly relaxed, behaving as though nothing of any significance had just happened.

But that interaction had profound consequences for LG. Although she did finally manage to rejoin the Talek clan several weeks later, she bore the bloody scars from this violent encounter for many months, and one of her two precious teats continued to dangle useless from her udder for the rest of her life. From that day forward, each time she produced a litter of two cubs, one of them was inevitably doomed to starve to death.

JOYCE POOLE | *Amboseli Elephant Research Project, Kenya*

Family Reunions

An African elephant mother named Ella and her teen-age daughter tend to Ella's new baby. Among elephants, caring for the young is a family affair, with sisters and aunts enthusiastically participating.

One of the strongest behavioral characteristics of African elephants is their demonstrative nature. Expressions of what appear to be joy, delight, silliness, and indignation are all commonly seen in the daily life of a family of elephants. Elephants seem to revel in making a "big deal" about everything. As a colleague of mine so aptly put it, they're Drama Queens. For example, if one member of a family expresses umbrage, family and friends rush to her side to comment and concur and to provide emotional support and physical backup, if necessary.

Expressions of joy and happiness are frequently observed within an elephant family. Perhaps the most notable such manifestations come during the greetings that are such an important part of elephant family life. These range from what I call Little Greetings, a soft rumble often exchanged between two closely bonded individuals, to the highly emotional Greeting Ceremony that may include as many as fifty elephants.

When individuals belonging to a family or bond-group have been separated for some time—perhaps hours, days, or weeks—the greeting becomes pandemonium. Members rush together, heads high, ears raised, folded, and flapping loudly, as they spin around urinating and defecating, and secreting profusely from their temporal glands. During all this activity they call in unison with a powerful sequence of low-frequency rumbles and higher-frequency screams, roars, and trumpets.

I've puzzled over these extraordinary greetings for many years. Is there a simple functional explanation for this remarkable cacophony of sound and scent? Could it be, for example, just an unemotional announcement to distant elephants that the unit is once again a force to be reckoned with? I don't accept, however, that the behavior of elephants is so mechanistic. I believe instead that greeting elephants feel a deep sense of joy at being reunited with friends and that their rumbles and roars express to one another something like: "Wow! It's simply fantastic to be with you again!"

My passionate view of elephant nature doesn't preclude a good evolutionary reason for their delight in one another's company. I believe that the joy female elephants feel when they reunite is real and that their feelings of well-being guide a response that's necessary for their survival. We know that calves born into large, closely knit families have a better chance of survival. We also know that strong and positive emotional responses between two adult females can build and reinforce the bond between them. Intense greetings are among the many ways in which elephants express their friendship and loyalty toward one another and renew the support network that's so important to their survival.

*A mother moose and her
week-old calf cross a
highway. Female moose
usually become fertile when
they're about two to three
years old. Thereafter, they
produce one or two calves a
year, although triplets are
not unheard of.*

Joel Berger | *University of Nevada, Reno*

Bones in the Snow

Moose, like cattle and even many native ungulates, are perceived by the public as big, slow feeding machines. Weighing up to three-quarters of a ton, moose consume massive amounts of woody vegetation to live through the brutally frigid arctic and subarctic winters. Starvation is not uncommon, and most deaths that are not at the hands of humans or vehicles or natural predation occur during winter.

One interesting adaptation is that the metabolic rates of moose drop during winter, so that despite increased energy needs, fewer calories are burned. Still, life is perilous for this asocial ungulate. Moose span the earth's circumpolar environments, dropping as far south as Mongolia in Asia and to the northern tiers of the Great Basin Desert in Nevada. An impressive cadre of nonhuman predators eat moose. They've been killed by orcas in the Pacific while swimming between islands in southeast Alaska, by tigers in China and Siberia, and by wolves and brown bears from Norway and Sweden to Canada and Alaska. But when moose colonized the Jackson Hole region south of Yellowstone National Park in Wyoming during the late 1800s, they entered a region that had lost most dangerous predators, and populations grew by more than twentyfold.

By 1990, concern about the burgeoning moose population's possible threat to sensitive

125

riparian zones was emerging, especially because most biodiversity in the arid western United States occurs in such environments. Four years later, my colleague Carol Cunningham and I began to study moose population ecology and behavior in Grand Teton National Park in Wyoming. There, the most potent death-dealers are gas-guzzling, environment-polluting vehicles (one of which I own).

In February 1998, a female moose we called Mother and her eight-month-old daughter left the safety of a thick willow patch in the center of their mountainous home range. The snow was already three feet deep at the time. Cars and eighteen-wheel trucks whizzed by at a hundred kilometers per hour, rupturing the frosty silence and spewing ice crystals in all directions. Adventurous tourists left the warmth of their cars for a few precious moments to point fingers, laugh, and photograph the pair, which had crossed this highway at least thirty times before. The next morning would be very different for Mother.

During the night she was hit by a powerful sport utility vehicle. Her pelvis crushed, she died two days later, about two hundred meters from the road. The calf was at her side. As biologists we're taught to be objective, to gather data without feelings, all in the spirit of science. So Carol tried to collect skeletal material from Mother, but the calf wouldn't leave the rigid body. Rather than cause the traumatized youngster more grief, Carol left, planning to return in a few days when the calf might be less

Moose are rather solitary animals. Very few live in groups of more than two, although groups of up to thirty-five can form temporarily in winter. Vehicles can claim many of their lives in some areas of Alaska.

attached. But even as coyotes and ravens and magpies were eating the insides out of Mother, the calf refused to depart. Even dead, Mother was the only source of protection and knowledge. Mother knew how to find the best food and how to avoid deadly humans, whether on foot or in cars. At some point, though, the calf would surely starve if it didn't leave her body.

Two weeks later, all that remained of Mother were patches of hair and a few bones, most of them buried under the latest snowfall. By now, however, not only was the calf no longer with the corpse, but there was no calf in sight. Two other biologists and I entered Mother's home range. Hoping to understand how maternal bonds affect the survival of offspring, we wanted to radio-collar the calf. This was science, where cold, snow, and orphaned calves mattered less than did the facts and figures used to test hypotheses.

On snowshoes and still sinking thigh-deep in snow on this minus-fourteen-degree-Fahrenheit morning, we spotted the calf almost a kilometer from the spot where Mother had died. As we approached to dart her with a tranquilizing drug, the terrified youngster ran and ran and ran. Plowing through chest-deep snow soon drained whatever energy she had left.

As we prepared to shoot, something glinted in the snow. We had lost our orientation, but the calf had not lost hers. There, mostly buried in deep snow, were skeletal remains, blood smears, and patches of hair. And that's where the calf stood. Remarkably, she had fought us and the snow to return to Mother, in what we could only interpret as a final hope for solace and protection, a hope

that somehow her dead mother would rear up and drive away us awful humans.

Indeed, the bond between the calf and Mother was strong. Could these animals really be only large feeding machines, bundles of endocrines driven by physiological desires? Were they uncaring and insensitive?

More than two months had passed since Mother's death. Winter's brutal grip had ended. It was May, and spring was palpable even in the Tetons. The sun shone and the air was warm. Melting water formed rivulets everywhere. Willows budded, migrant birds appeared, and the riparian zones were alive and full of seasonal beauty. Unlike six other orphans that had died, our calf fed near Mother's body and still wore her radio-collar.

We all celebrated, feeling this would be the one to make it. Two weeks later, she was dead of starvation.

CLINTON R. SANDERS | *University of Connecticut*

Simple Pleasures

Clint Sanders and two of
his Newfoundlands, Isis
and Raven, enjoy one of
their daily walks in the
Connecticut woods. His
dogs, like most, are adept
at studying the facial
expressions of their human
and canine companions
to gauge moods, emotions,
and intentions.

In the decade that I've spent exploring the practical and emotional connections between people and their dogs, what I've come to know most clearly is that humans see their dog companions as unique individuals who are both thoughtful and emotional. As with our intimate human associations, understanding and sharing a canine companion's outlook and experience is the foundation for a mutually fulfilling relationship. Understanding your dog's special joys and fears is central to knowing his or her personality, and is the foundation for the love that exists between person and dog.

Quite early in our relationship I learned, for example, that more than almost anything, my Newfoundland Shadow loved to chase, carry, and swim after sticks that she chose for herself. Her older half-sister Raven, by way of contrast, couldn't have cared less about sticks and seemed to regard Shadow's passion for them with amused tolerance. Both Raven and Shadow, on the other hand, respond with happy anticipation when they hear me running the hair dryer, since they know this means I'll soon be off to work and they'll receive that most wonderful of treats, a handful of popcorn from the jar on the kitchen counter. I'd have to be a very stupid interactant were I not able to understand the basic joy they feel, since their actions—upright postures, prancing, waving tails—are at least as eloquent as mere words could be.

The joy my dogs communicate to me offers an important lesson. When I see the happiness they derive from a walk in the woods, a meal provided at the usual time, the warmth of a body to press against on a cold evening, I realize that the basic and immediate pleasures are the most important and should be treasured.

Like my own experience with my dogs, my research into the social bond between them and us has consistently shown me the importance of the joy they feel and regularly demonstrate in maintenance of our relationship. For people who depend on dogs for special assistance, knowing their animal companions' thought processes and feelings is central to building an effective alliance. The visually impaired people with whom I talked when studying a guide dog training program often spoke of the special pleasure their dogs derived from doing the work they were trained for—and, in contrast, the embarrassment they obviously felt when they made mistakes.

Here is the core of our intimate relationships with dogs: We understand their emotions and draw from our experiences with them the knowledge that they can, in turn, feel something of what we feel. As in our relationships with special people, dog caretakers cherish the happiness their dogs experience, since it's the foundation of the intense emotional connectedness we humans refer to as love.

FRANCINE L. DOLINS | *Polytechnic University, New York*
AND CHRISTOPHER G. KLIMOWICZ

Tag in the Treetops

Our distant cousins, lemurs are classified as prosimians, meaning that they evolved earlier than the anthropoid primates—monkeys, apes, and humans. Found only on the island of Madagascar and their numbers shrinking as human habitats encroach on theirs, lemurs are among the most endangered primates in the world.

What is joy when expressed in play? Although hard to define, it's immediately recognizable, even in species very different from humans. It was abundantly obvious, for instance, during the time we spent in Ranomafana National Park, Madagascar, studying the red-fronted brown lemurs (*Eulemur fulvus rufous*) that live in the forests there.

One day we observed two youngsters in the group in a bout of particularly vibrant and unrestrained play amid a contingent of napping adults. Two of the adults, Lulu and Fred, were among those resting after a morning's foraging, lying close together for warmth in the damp winter air. A juvenile, Ketchme, was playing chase with a neighbor's kid, Beanie, running up and down, swinging energetically from branch to branch, barely avoiding huddled pairs of resting adults scattered here and there in the trees. In contrast to the inert grownups, the two juveniles were wildly exuberant in their gymnastic swoops and leaps.

At last, perhaps from sheer exhaustion, the youngsters seemed to be slowing down. But just then Ketchme passed under the adults' prone forms. On the run, hotly pursued by Beanie, she gave a rapid tug to a hanging object, which turned out to be Fred's long tail. He nearly fell out of the V of the tree branches, emitting grunts of displeasure. Regaining his balance, Fred shook himself and glared around, then curled around Lulu to begin his rest once more. A few trees down, Ketchme and Beanie, their energy renewed, were in a rough-and-tumble roll, almost dislodging each other from the high branches. From such a height, a sheer fall was possible. But if they were mindful of the danger they also seemed careless of it, lost in the sheer joy of play.

Françoise Wemelsfelder | *Scottish Agricultural College, Edinburgh*

Lives of Quiet Desperation

This pig's posture is typical of an animal who's become apathetic and lethargic. The hunched back, drooping head and ears, and half-closed eyes all speak of the helplessness pigs can feel when penned in small, barren cages.

Biological science tends to assume that we can't know directly what an animal feels, that emotions are hidden within the animal's brain. But I believe this view unnecessarily creates a split between body and mind, between behavior and emotion. Animals are integrated beings whose behavior has an expressive quality, a body language that speaks to us in a meaningful way. Animals can behave fearfully, confidently, apathetically, excitedly, or calmly. In the way in which an animal acts and moves about, its experience of a situation is present for us to observe and share. It's possible, of course, to make mistakes; to correctly interpret an animal's behavioral expression, we have to be well acquainted with a particular creature and with the species it belongs to. With enough experience, however, we can get it right.

In my work I meet mostly pigs, which are naturally inquisitive and alert animals. If I enter a pen with young pigs, after a moment's hesitation they quickly approach and vigorously sniff and nibble my hand. But they're also quick to withdraw; one unexpected movement from me and they back away. Newborn piglets are in danger of being crushed by the sow, so picking up a young pig or holding it for a moment will cause it to scream at the top of its lungs and to frantically wriggle to get away. Such behavior helps the piglet survive, but it also conveys panic and acute despair. For us, this may seem exaggerated in a situation of mild and harmless restraint. From the pig's point of view, however, the despair is very real. That most pigs calm down as soon as they are freed is no reason for us to suspect that the previous moment of despair wasn't intense.

In the highly restrictive and monotonous agricultural environments in which we keep pigs, their alert responsiveness may disappear and give way to drowsy lethargy. I gained a clear impression of this in a young female pig that had been housed alone for many months in a small barren pen. She was sitting on the floor, her hind legs stretched underneath her, her back hunched, her head and ears drooping, and her tongue occasionally hanging out of her mouth. She had been sitting this way for quite some time, and my entrance into the pen had little effect. When I sat down next to her and carefully touched her, she glanced at me but didn't move. As the moments passed, I was struck by the soft, gentle, helpless quality of her passivity, the total absence of hostility, fear, or any other active response. She was present only vaguely, her apathy such a stark contrast to what pigs normally are like.

What I realized that day is that the expression of suffering, in pigs and perhaps in

other animals as well, is not necessarily dramatic or assertive. It can take the form of withdrawal, of absence rather than presence, and it can appear in an expression so subtle that we could easily fail to notice it or, having noticed, ignore its significance. Yet the soft quality of a pig's helplessness signals a suffering that is serious rather than slight. It speaks of a loss of communication, of a lost ability to cope. I found the quiet emptiness emanating from the pig poignant and very sad.

It seems to me that animal suffering is invisible only when we avert our eyes. With prolonged and careful observation, the nature of that suffering is bound to become clear.

CYNTHIA MOSS | *African Wildlife Foundation*

A Passionate Devotion

With an animal as slow to reproduce as an elephant, it's not surprising that a mother invests a great deal of time and energy in the single calf that she bears once every four to five years. The evidence is there in the twenty-two months of gestation and in the four years or even more of lactation. What's harder to quantify, if not impossible, is the emotional energy a female expends in her relationship with her calf.

I have no doubt that elephant mothers feel very strongly about their young; the intense attachment is evident in their maternal behavior. But what does the female feel when she suckles her calf, or rescues it when it falls in a water hole, or lifts it to its feet when it's weak, or carries it on her trunk and tusks when it's dying? It's easy to say that she simply reacts instinctively to the calf's vocalizations and behavior. True, but what does she feel when she reacts? Elephants eat when they feel hungry, drink when they feel thirsty, run when they feel frightened, scream when they feel pain. Is it such a leap to say that as an elephant gently touches her calf with her trunk, she feels love?

In 1990, I was making a film in Kenya about a single family of elephants, the EBs, led by a beautiful matriarch, Echo. She was due to have a calf in late February. On the morning of February 28, cameraman Martyn Colbeck and I found the EB family shortly after dawn with a brand new calf. It was a male, and it was Echo's.

Martyn started filming, but we soon realized that there was something wrong with the calf. He couldn't stand because his front legs were bent and rigid at the carpal joints. Echo kept reaching her trunk around and under the calf, wedging a toe under him, and lifting. He was big and strong; he could get up on his hind legs. But then all he could do was shuffle around on his "knees" until he collapsed again. Over and over she tried to lift him, but he could not walk.

Eventually, most of the fourteen-member family left, but Echo and one of her daughters, nine-year-old Enid, stayed with the calf. Enid also tried to lift him, but Echo gently pushed her away. Once the calf was half standing, Enid came up beside him and started walking away, looking back, apparently trying to make him follow. He couldn't.

By now it was hot, and the three elephants were out in the open with no shade, no food, and no water. Patiently and very slowly they managed to move to a small mud hole where Echo and Enid splashed themselves and the calf. By midafternoon they were doubtless extremely hungry and thirsty, but neither female would leave. The calf was exhausted; when Echo tried again to get him to his feet, he screamed. Frequently both Echo and Enid made the low, rumbling contact call to the rest of the family, listened for an answer, then

An adult female elephant gently helps an infant to its feet. Newborn elephants are quite sturdy creatures, standing about three feet at the shoulder and weighing some 200 pounds. Despite their size, they are completely dependent on their mother and other family members.

answered in turn. Enid moved off, turned back, moved off again, her behavior suggesting intense conflict. At one point she got about thirty meters away, but just then Echo tried to get the calf to his feet again and he bellowed. Enid spun around and rushed back to him.

By the end of the day we had little hope for the calf. He was just able to reach Echo's breast from an awkward position, but he could not sustain it for long. Amazingly, he survived the night, and over the next two days he learned how to shuffle along on his carpal joints with Echo and Enid on either side, moving slowly, stopping often. On the second day there was a tiny bit of movement in his joints. On the third day Martyn filmed him as he stood for the first time. I don't know what Echo was feeling, but Martyn wept—both for Echo, for her commitment and tenderness, and for the calf, for his courage and determination.

Later I named the calf Ely, and as I write this today he is almost ten years old. He's had several mishaps, but the most serious occurred just after he turned seven. I was having a shower one afternoon when Echo and the family arrived at the little swamp behind me. A friend who came over to watch them noticed that there was something sticking out of Ely's back. She got her binoculars, and we saw that it was a spear made of twisted metal. About a foot was imbedded in his back, and three feet were sticking out. He was bleeding.

The next morning I flew to Nairobi and went straight to the Kenya Wildlife Service headquarters. A few days later they were able to send a vet team to Amboseli to try to treat Ely.

What struck everyone during the procedure was Echo's behavior. By now she had another calf, a three-year-old, but her bond with Ely was clearly still very strong. The team had a terrible time keeping her from trying to rescue her son.

The whole family had panicked when Ely went down under a tranquilizer. His kin surrounded him and desperately tried to lift him. The vet team tried to chase them off. After a brave showing, several of the elephants ran. Finally, only Echo and two of her daughters, Enid and Eliot, remained. They refused to leave, even in the face of vehicles driving full-speed toward them and gunshots being fired over their heads. Finally, one of my research colleagues managed to keep Echo at bay with a Land Rover, but she stood right next to his vehicle, making a groove in the door with her tusk while the vets worked on Ely—successfully, I'm happy to report.

Iain Douglas-Hamilton, who was in Amboseli making a documentary, told me that for him, Echo's response, her courage and passion, epitomized all that's extraordinary about elephants. While he watched her risk her life for her calf, he, like Martyn seven years before, had tears running down his face.

DENISE L. HERZING | *Florida Atlantic University*

A Trail of Grief

Dolphins invest a lot of time and care in their babies. Depending on the species, gestation can take eleven to twelve months before the mother gives birth to a single calf. The youngster will stay with her, continuing to nurse, for three to four years or until the mother gives birth again.

Long-term bonding is especially strong in dolphin society. Dolphins play, travel, fight, and forage together, forging close relationships with family and friends.

I arrived in the Bahamas in 1985 to study Atlantic spotted dolphins. Among the first I met were Rosemole, Little Gash, and Mugsy, three juvenile females in the middle of their childhood years. Their days were spent playing, traveling, and sometimes interacting with we humans who were trying to observe them underwater. As the years passed, all three females became engaged in courtship and mating with the ever-persistent maturing male spotted dolphins. By 1990, both Rosemole and Mugsy were pregnant for the first time. First parturition is a critical time, one in which female dolphins test their relationships with one another, bonding with others of the same reproductive status. In the case of Rosemole and Mugsy, they were already strong friends.

My field season runs through the summer, and by its end in 1990, both Rosemole and Mugsy were bulging with offspring that would probably be born in the spring. As I left in the fall, I thought how exciting it would be to come back the next year and see both these females

that I'd grown up with during the last five years with their first babies.

The following May we returned to our field site and met up with a mother/calf group that included both Rosemole and Mugsy. Rosemole had a healthy young female baby, Rosebud, and they were surrounded by other mothers who proudly swam along with their calves. But on the periphery was Mugsy, in formation but without a calf. She might have had a miscarriage or lost her calf, either to a predator or from natural causes. Swimming slowly and despondently on the edge of the group, she stayed in line but left a space beneath her, as though she had a phantom calf in tow. She showed no interest in her friends or in mating again. Month after month Mugsy left her trail of grief, as clear as a luminescent streak in the dark water.

The grieving process isn't unique to mothers and their first offspring; it's also strong in mothers who have multiple young. The previous year I had observed a lone dolphin swimming on a shipwreck we often use for anchorage. On approaching her, I saw that she had a large shark bite above her left pectoral fin. She was emaciated, and a remora was clinging to her. Her swimming appeared despondent and disoriented. It's very unusual to see a dolphin swimming alone, except when one is sick or wounded. Days later, I reviewed my videotape

and realized that this individual was one I knew well but hadn't recognized at the time. It was Gemini, mother of a three-year-old, Gemer.

Gemer had been a spunky little dolphin, and we'd often recognized her partly by the presence of a telltale remora, a clingy fish, that was always with her. But now there was no Gemer with Gemini, nor was the baby ever seen again. Defending her offspring, Gemini had likely done battle with a predator. Perhaps she'd lost Gemer in the fray, and the remora once attached to the baby had switched to the wounded mother.

It's amazing Gemini survived at all, mourning and wounded as she was, and emaciated from the inability or unwillingness to eat. Her wounds eventually healed, however, and she regained her weight and went on to have two more healthy calves. Grief had been experienced and processed, and life had returned to the business of renewal, a new chance at life.

JANE GOODALL | *Explorer-in-residence, National Geographic Society*

A Sorrow Beyond Tears

Chimpanzees, differing from us genetically by only just over one percent, can't be said to weep, for they don't shed tears. Yet they show behavior that's associated with sadness, depression, and grief in humans: soft whimpering, crying sounds, listlessness, lack of appetite, avoidance of others. And they show those behaviors in the same kind of situations that we do.

In 1972, in Africa's Gombe National Park, the almost fifty-year-old matriarch of our study community died. Flo, as she was called, was with her eight-and-a-half-year-old son, Flint. He should have been able to look after himself, easily. Yet he'd developed a strange, abnormal dependence on his old mother, probably because she hadn't had the energy to wean him properly. All day he sat near her body at the edge of a small, fast-flowing stream. Occasionally he approached her, inspecting her carefully, moving all around, then grooming her a little. He pulled her dead hand toward him, whimpering; in life she had responded, grooming him in return. Then he moved a few yards away to sit, hunched and motionless, eyes staring. As darkness fell, Flint climbed into a tree and made a small nest—to spend the first night of his life alone.

RIGHT: *Flint stares into space in deep depression over his mother's death.*
ABOVE: *Flint's mother, Flo, with one of her offspring.*

On the second day Flint heard his brother calling in a nearby group, and he joined them. Some of his depression lifted for a while, but after a few hours he suddenly left the other chimps and hurried back to the place where Flo had died. There he sat alone, eyes staring into space. Later he climbed slowly into a tall tree, walked along a branch, and stood staring at a large empty nest—the one that Flo had made and that he and she had slept in the previous week. What was he thinking? He climbed down and lay on the ground, staring at nothing.

Over the next three weeks, Flint became increasingly lethargic. He stopped eating, and he avoided other chimps, huddling in the vegetation close to where he'd last seen Flo. His eyes sank deep into the hollow sockets of his skull; his movements were like an old man's. The last short journey he made, with many pauses, was to the very place where Flo's body had lain. There he remained, sometimes staring and staring into the water, until he died, just three and a half weeks after losing Flo. He died of grief.

Joyce Poole | *Amboseli Elephant Research Project, Kenya*

When Bonds Are Broken

Solemn and silent, elephants gather around the bones of one of their fellows. In the presence of their dead, elephants may spend up to an hour touching and turning the bones with their trunks and feet. Sometimes they carry the bones away with them.

Much has been written about how elephants react to the death or injury of one of their own, or even to the presence of elephant remains. Their behavior around their dead is silent and contemplative, leaving me with little doubt that they experience deep emotions and have some understanding of death.

Elephants are particularly interested in tusks and may carry them long distances before dropping them, but they also carry other bones. I once watched an elephant walk off with a newly collected lower jaw that was part of a scientific assemblage. Other naturalists have observed an elephant returning bones to the original site of an animal's death, and moving and burying scores of elephant feet and ears that were drying after a culling operation.

Elephants have been seen trying to feed a dying elephant and to cover dead ones with vegetation. They also try to raise immobilized, injured, dying, or dead companions. So strong is this tendency among family members that when an elephant has to be immobilized for research or medical purposes, its kin often must be chased away.

Some years ago, I witnessed the death of an elephant named Polly and watched as three males spent an hour trying to raise or revive her.

Using their trunks, they tried to pull her up by her own trunk, her tusks, and her tail; with their tusks and their feet they tried to lift her; and eventually the largest of the three males mounted her more than twenty times. Two days later, after rangers had hacked Polly's long, asymmetrical tusks from her face, I returned to find the same three males standing side by side, touching her mutilated face with their trunks, undoubtedly able to detect the hand of man. They were deeply engrossed in their investigation, and I had the horrible realization that on some level they understood the connection between Polly's wounds and the missing tusks.

On a couple of occasions I've seen very real grief on the faces of elephants. The first time was when I watched a young female, Tonie, stand guard over her stillborn baby for three days. The first day she tried over and over to revive him by lifting him with her trunk, tusks, and forefoot. Then, she simply stood by him. Throughout, her face and body expressed what I recognized from my own experience as grief. Her head, ears, and trunk drooped, the corners of her mouth turned down, and her movements were quiet and slow. I knew that Tonie was experiencing a deep sense of loss.

More recently, I testified in a cruelty case in a South African court on behalf of thirty baby elephants who had had been forcibly taken from their families in the wild. Aged two to

seven years old and destined for zoos and safari parks around the world, these babies were undergoing traditional methods of "training" that involved beatings and other punishment. What I saw in their posture and facial expressions appalled me. Their eyes looked dark and hollow, alternately wide and fearful or downcast and empty. Their mouths either gaped in terror or turned down in grief. Their heads and ears were high and alert one minute, hanging listlessly the next. Their skin was dull and mottled. When the youngsters were unchained, they didn't play with one another as young elephants usually do, but shuffled in leaderless groups or wandered listlessly about.

Is there a good evolutionary argument for elephants being able to experience grief and despair? Every elephant calf is biologically extremely important to its mother, because she must invest so much time, energy, and effort in producing and rearing it. Elephants have, therefore, evolved elaborate behaviors to care for and bond with their calves. If a calf is to survive, it, too, must form an intense bond with its mother and other family members. In fact, the survival of all elephants depends on maintaining strong ties within their social network. It would be odd indeed if they did not feel grief when the bonds are broken.

Naomi A. Rose | *The Humane Society of the United States*

A Death in the Family

Whatever the cause of this beached orca's death, it leaves close-knit family members behind. Orca families travel, and even rest, together. The lifelong bond between mothers and sons is extremely rare among mammals.

In late November of 1990, A9 died. She was an older orca, in her sixth decade. When she was younger, she must have been run over by the propeller of a large vessel; she had a deep, healed-over gash just forward of her tail flukes—the cut had nearly severed them from her body—and a shallower gash behind her dorsal fin. The fin, too, had been damaged. She was known as Scar.

Scar was always accompanied by two male orcas. Researchers believed them to be her sons, the younger one an older adolescent, the older one a young adult. Scar and her sons had been identified as individuals since at least the early 1970s. The elder son was called Top Notch because of the perfect melon-scoop of a nick at the top of his tall, triangular dorsal fin. He was known more formally as A5, his brother as A26.

Whale watchers noted the presence of the trio in Johnstone Strait in mid-November 1990. In late November, Scar's body was discovered on a beach near Hanson Island, already several days gone. It's rare for researchers to recover the body of an orca in the Inside Passage; an animal simply disappears and is presumed dead. Not only was there a body in this case, but Scar had been seen alive within days of the body's discovery. That's as precise a time of death as one can hope for with these marine mammals.

For a day or two following her death, Scar's sons swam together, visiting again and again the places their mother had passed in the last few days of her life. They were alone. Whether they were avoiding others or others were avoiding them is impossible to say. But the steady swimming of these two animals, retracing the movements of their mother during her final days, seemed expressive of grief to me. They were holding a lonely vigil, perhaps honoring her, perhaps desperately searching for her. Or perhaps simply fixing her in their memory. Whatever its intent, the ritual went on for a couple of days before the two males disappeared from the area. For a while, it was feared they, too, were dead. But eventually, weeks later, they returned to Johnstone Strait.

Top Notch and his younger brother are still alive almost a decade later, still swimming side by side. They do associate occasionally with other whales in their pod, but they are often seen alone.

JAAK PANKSEPP | *Bowling Green State University*

The Rat Will Play

Adult rats show a keen social interest in one another, with abundant mutual grooming. Although roughhouse play declines as rats age, they still direct their socializing toward bodily areas that were the most common targets of play during youth—face to face, for instance.

All mammals play spontaneously when they're young. They don't need to learn to play, but they'll do it only when they have a secure emotional base. Some people feel that the lowly rat has no playful nature, nor any other redeeming qualities, but they're so wrong. Anyone who's ever had young rats for pets knows that they're delightful and loving creatures. And if they have no other companions, they enjoy playing with humans very much indeed.

As a student I had a pet rat named Tulip. Coming out to greet me whenever I returned home, she was especially eager for a little game wherein I'd toss her gently from one end of a couch to the other. She'd eagerly scurry back for more and more of this fun. I usually tired of it long before she did.

We've now studied rough-and-tumble play in young rats for a few decades, and we remain delighted by their antics and their deep desire for romping. Indeed, rats even chirp with joy when they're playing. When we started to listen carefully to the sounds they made during play—sounds inaudible to us without special equipment—the air was filled with short, high-frequency vocalizations (~fifty-kilohertz chirps). Rats continue to make such sounds during positive social engagements as adults, but at much lower levels. They also chirp a lot when they're anticipating various treats, including drugs that humans commonly abuse. They make no such sounds when negative events occur; rather, they exhibit prolonged twenty-two-kilohertz "complaints."

A few years ago, we started to suspect that chirping in rats was a kind of primitive laughter. When we tickled our rats, especially at the nape of the neck where they typically initiate play with one another, they chirped at remarkably high levels. They thoroughly enjoyed being tickled and became especially fond of hands that tickled them, while showing no special preference for hands that merely petted them. When we tickled them, the rats also tried to reciprocate—to play with us. They gently nipped our fingers, especially if we paused in our play, apparently in an attempt to solicit more. I've been "bitten" thousands of times by young rats, but never seriously. Just like puppies or kittens, they never break the skin in their playful eagerness. It's through tickling and other play that they get friendly with others and thereby learn a great deal about their social world.

As every young child knows, play is the very source of joy, and there should be little doubt that rats feel such positive emotions, as

do all mammals. Just as our human choices are dictated usually by what makes us feel good or bad, every indication is that other animals base their choices on the same criteria. They seek out what makes them feel good, and they avoid what makes them feel bad. This may seem to be a simple and self-evident fact, but it's also a profound truth of nature. It's a pity that so many scientists who use animals in their research often refuse to acknowledge such a fundamental truth. Their research would improve enormously, and our understanding of

animals would progress more rapidly, if scientists were more willing to consider that evolution built emotions into the nervous system at the very foundation of that mysterious process we call consciousness. This is not to say, of course, that other animals cognitively appreciate and dwell on their own feelings the way humans do. That may require more cortex in higher brain regions than most other animals have.

RUTH C. NEWBERRY | *Washington State University*

The Joy of Bathing

I have been studying the behavior of chickens for more than fifteen years. One aspect that I especially enjoy observing is dust bathing. I think this is because the activity appears to be so eminently pleasant for the chickens, and their joy is contagious.

Whereas some birds use water to clean themselves, chickens use dust. They find a place with dry, fine soil, and then they peck and scratch at it for a few minutes. They may do this together with their flockmates; dust bathing is often a social affair that takes place in a communal bathing site.

If the site is suitable and there's no sign of danger, the chickens squat down and use their wings to scoop dust up into their feathers. While making rapid vertical movements with their wings, they fluff up their feathers, allowing the dust to percolate down to the skin. Once the feathers are saturated, the birds flatten them, trapping the dust.

Fully dusted, a chicken will lie quietly in the shallow hollow created by its bathing movements, often leaning to one side with its upper leg extended. If undisturbed, it may loll like this for twenty minutes or more, occasionally rubbing its head in the soil, turning over, or adjusting its position with a few pushes of the outstretched leg. The bath ends when the bird gets up, takes a few steps away, and vigorously shakes all of the dust out of its feathers.

Why do chickens dust bathe? One benefit is that it fluffs up the downy portion of the feathers, improving the insulating quality. Another plus is that it removes old, stale oil from the feathers. The dust absorbs the oil, and when the birds shake off the dust, the oil goes with it. When roosting in a safe place after bathing, the birds can apply fresh oil to their feathers. They have an oil gland on the upper base of their tail that looks like a short stalk with a ring of bristles around the tip. They reach around and manipulate the gland with their beak to get some oil, then they run the beak through the feathers to distribute it. This waterproofing oil keeps them dry and also keeps their flight feathers in working order.

Dust bathing has persisted in chickens despite generations of artificial selection. Even naked chickens that have a genetic mutation eliminating feather growth go through the motions of dust bathing. However, chickens that have never had the opportunity to dust bathe might never attempt it. If they're living indoors, protected from the elements, they may not suffer from this blank space in their behavioral repertoire. On the other hand, once chickens have experienced the pleasure of dust bathing, they have a strong desire to keep doing it.

A nice wallow in the dust (or some suitably dry equivalent) is a chicken's idea of a good time. Dust bathing helps keep them clean and warm.

I've tried to satisfy this desire by providing caged laying hens with a plastic box containing fine sand. Hens are typically kept in cages for commercial egg production, because the eggs roll out of the cages as soon as they're laid. This affords a reliable way of collecting all the eggs and ensuring that they're fresh, clean, and intact. I found that if I left the sandbox in the cage all the time, the sand disappeared rapidly, the box quickly became dirty, and the hens laid eggs in it. These eggs got soiled and were sometimes cracked by the hens. Some of the birds even learned to break them open and eat them.

Previous research has shown that hens kept in pens on litter-covered floors dust bathe about once every three to four days. I tried providing the sandbox to the caged birds every two to three days, but even this short interval left them seemingly desperate for a bath. When I

placed the box in the cage, all the birds scrambled furiously to get inside. In some groups, the alpha hen aggressively prevented the other birds from using the sandbox. In other groups, the scrambling birds quickly depleted the sand, and none got a proper bath.

Recently, the European Union decided to ban the use of existing cage designs for housing laying hens. As of 2012, hens kept in cages must be provided with a perch, a nest, and a littered area in which they can dust bathe. It'll be interesting to see how this works out. Research is needed to ensure that this well-intentioned legislation actually improves the well-being of the birds, allowing them, among other things, the joy of dust bathing.

The bond between a female olive baboon and her offspring is very strong. Newborns are carried on the mother's belly. Older infants, like this one, hitch rides on mother's back.

Barbara Smuts | *University of Michigan*

Child of Mine

More than thirty years ago, psychologists separated baby rhesus monkeys from their mothers to see if they could create an animal model of human grief. They found that monkeys who lost their mothers showed many of the physiological changes that characterize depressed humans. Their sleep suffered and their immune systems broke down, which made them more vulnerable to illness. But most convincing were the heart-wrenching photographs of monkey babies whose large eyes held the dazed expression of trauma victims.

While studying wild baboons in Kenya, I met such an infant. Near the research station where I lived, an adult female baboon was found dead in a poacher's snare. Her baby, cloaked in the velvety black fur of newborns, was still clinging to his mother's cold body. Another researcher brought the baby home, fed him milk, put him in a cage in a warm room, and then forgot about him. I stumbled over him the next morning.

He was barely alive. His eyes were cloudy, unfocused, and swollen half shut. His body was cold, his breathing almost undetectable. I removed him from the cage, remembering all I'd learned about how infant primates respond to maternal loss. I held him close, groomed him, and carried him everywhere for the rest of the day. Although I thought he was too ill to make it through the night, I wanted to comfort him

151

during his last hours. That evening he went to sleep lying on my chest, his head against my heart. In the middle of the night I was awakened by a rambunctious baby baboon who wanted to play!

The next morning, clear-eyed, he stayed close to me, venturing only a few cautious steps away when I sat down. But if I removed him when he was clinging to me, he threw a tantrum, writhing on the ground and screaming, just as baboon infants do with their mothers. And like the baboon mothers, I couldn't bear his suffering, so I would pick him up again. Immediately calm, he would then gaze at me with utter devotion.

I named the little guy Hilary, and my fears for his future were relieved when he was adopted by a friend of mine who could be with him around the clock. He developed a strong bond with her, and he set about enjoying what at least a few people regarded as a fully human existence: When we took Hilary to the Nairobi drive-in, we had to pay for him. In response to our protests, we were told, "Well, he's going to watch the movie, isn't he?" And in fact he did.

Sadly, a few weeks later Hilary died in his sleep of sudden infant death syndrome. But I'll never forget him or the lesson he taught me: A few hours of tender body contact can miraculously transform looming death to exuberant life.

Later I saw how a mother baboon reacts to losing her infant. Zandra, a high-ranking

female, became briefly separated from her six-month-old baby. She was searching for Zephyr frantically when we heard high-pitched screams. We found Zephyr's body seconds later with two deep puncture wounds in the skull. The killer, a male new to the troop, was leaving the scene of the crime. Zandra clutched Zephyr's body for hours (a common response of primate mothers whose infants have died). While carrying the corpse, she kept trying to peer at other infants clinging to their mothers. It was clear to me that she wanted only to gaze at a living infant and meant no harm, but the other mothers avoided her because she was such a dominant animal. She ended up watching babies from a distance, grunting to them softly whenever she made eye contact.

The next day, Zandra no longer carried the body and seemed to be back to normal. But a month later, when the troop passed through the same area where she'd lost her baby, Zandra immediately began climbing trees and looking all around her, uttering the same call she'd given when searching for Zephyr. She hadn't forgotten her loss after all.

The most surprising and poignant reaction to infant loss I ever saw, however, involved not baboons but an elegant African antelope the size of a half-grown deer. One morning, my colleague Richard Wrangham and I came upon four adult male baboons chasing an infant female impala. Pala, as we called her mother, chased one male up a tree and forced another to drop the baby, which he held clutched in his jaws. But a third attacker grabbed the tiny antelope and killed her. It was excruciating to watch Pala, a few meters away, staring intently while the baboon ate her baby. When he moved away, satiated, she chased him briefly, then returned to gaze at her infant's half-eaten body.

We moved off with the baboons, but when we returned in the late afternoon, Pala was still standing motionless over the body, perhaps guarding it from further harm. The next morning we found her in the same spot, eyes riveted to the ground, as if the intensity of her longing might animate the bones. When we came back later that day, she was gone. Perhaps Pala had been in shock for twenty-four hours, or perhaps the silent vigil was simply her way of mourning the loss of her child.

Some people argue that only humans know emotional pain. Others acknowledge that perhaps nonhuman primates suffer, but they remain convinced that less brainy creatures, like rodents or ungulates, do not. I hope that stories like Pala's might help change their minds.

MARC BEKOFF | *University of Colorado, Boulder*

Missing Mother

A coyote cub tumbles happily between her mother's paws while her sibling and mom "jaw wrestle," an affectionate form of play. Parents and cubs often mouth one another in this way for long periods of time near the safety of their den.

For seven years, my students and I studied the social behavior of coyotes around Blacktail Butte in Wyoming's Grand Teton National Park. A female we called Mom was a mother and mate from the beginning of the study until late 1980, when she began leaving her family for short forays. She would disappear for a few hours and then return to the pack as if nothing strange had happened. I wondered if her family missed her when she wandered off. It certainly seemed that they did.

Mom's forays grew longer and longer, often lasting for a day or two at a time, and some pack members began looking at her curiously before she left. They would cock their heads to the side and squint their eyes and furrow their brows as if to ask, "Where are you going now?" Some of her children would even follow her for a while.

In Mom's absence the other pack members were unusually quiet, often looking toward the direction where she had disappeared. When she returned to the group, they greeted her effusively, whining loudly, licking her muzzle, wagging their tails like windmills, and rolling over gleefully in front of her. Their sadness instantly turned to joy.

But one day she left and never returned. The pack waited impatiently for days. Some coyotes paced, nervous as expectant parents, while others went off on short trips, only to return alone. They traveled in the direction she had gone, sniffed in places she might have visited, and howled as if calling her home. For more than a week some spark seemed to have vanished from the pack.

It was clear to all of us that coyotes, like many other animals, have deep and complicated feelings. They were sad, some on the verge of grieving. Their behavior told it all. They walked around with tails and heads drooping low, despondent over their loss.

After a while, though, life returned to normal on Blacktail Butte: Sleep, eat, play a little, hunt, defend the territory, rest, travel. A new female joined the pack, was accepted, formed a partnership with the breeding dominant male, and eventually gave birth to eight babies. She was now mom and mate.

But every now and again it seemed that some of the pack members still missed the original Mom. Maybe she was lost, maybe she would return if they went to look for her. They would sit up, look around, raise their noses to the wind, head off on short trips in the direction that she'd last traveled, and return weary without her. These searches went on for three or four months, but finally they ended. Pack members still seemed to miss Mom, but enough was enough. There were things to be done that couldn't be put off any longer.

MAREK ŠPINKA | *Research Institute of Animal Production, Prague, Czech Republic*

They Just Wanna Have Fun

A scampering piglet seems to delight in its own speed. Energetic, affectionate, and curious, little pigs sometimes bark from excitement as they play.

Pigs are misunderstood. Scorned by many people as smelly, dirty, even malicious animals, domestic pigs are, in fact, clever, sensitive, highly sociable, and emotional. Their every behavior is full of passion.

They're passionate, for instance, about play. Even in the barren settings of industrial farms, young pigs play long, hard, and often. The joy they derive from playing is obvious in the vitality of their scampering, chasing, and pivoting.

Consider this: A piglet, standing tense on all fours, suddenly tosses its head violently from side to side. You can't appreciate the speed of this movement with the naked eye, but on twenty-five-frames-per-second video you see the huge angular acceleration that smears the image of the piglet's head on individual frames. Before the tossing ends, the piglet leaps into a scamper. Each jump follows a highly arched trajectory and is accompanied by an up-and-down nodding of the head. The piglet covers several meters, changing the direction here and there. The performance continues with a powerful, 360-degree pivot: With its legs propelling a sideways launch, it twists right and left, bending its body almost at right angles. Directly from this half-flying body rotation, it lands on its belly, its front paws and chin on the floor, and there it freezes. But its eyes roll left and right,

as though to ask, "Is somebody following me?" Or maybe, "Did you see that?"

On slow-motion video, the movements of this sequence show striking amplitude, force, and angular speed. Seen in real time, the play looks impressively joyful and irresistibly funny, especially against the background of littermates frolicking in their own original romps.

Most people would agree that playing piglets probably feel something positive. But exactly what kind of experience is it? Is it the exhilarating, rewarding, yet lighthearted feeling that we humans have during physical play? Or, as some skeptics claim, is it just a crude positive urge to "seek this" (as opposed to the negative "avoid that") that makes them play? Scientific evidence suggests that play is connected with a specific emotion shared by different mammalian species.

My most persuasive personal experience along this line was with Tarash, a young female Belgian shepherd. She's a vivid, uninhibited, self-confident, and very sociable character. When she first arrived at our lab with her owner, one of my colleagues, she immediately wanted to play with Ajvik, a good-natured, thirteen-year-old Airedale. Tarash scampered, pounced, jumped, swiveled, and froze. Her play bows were flawless. Ajvik was kind, but lacking her agility, he soon left the room. Tarash looked

around for another playmate. I needed a break from the computer, so I volunteered to play.

I stared at her, then jerked suddenly to one side. Reacting instantly, Tarash jumped sideways, described a small semicircle, and stopped, waiting for my next move. I lunged for her, but she was off and running, inviting me to chase. So we chased for a while, she always leading, stopping only to permit an occasional touch.

I felt awkward running in my upright position, and slow in changing directions. But I enjoyed watching Tarash and inciting her lightning escapes. Since that day, we've often chased though the interconnecting rooms on the institute's ground floor. Once, trying to hide from her, I crouched behind a desk, only to turn and find her already there, staring right into my face. I took several playful swats at her muzzle, unsure whether I was demonstrating scientific curiosity or merely mimicking a gesture that many mammals use in play. In any case, Tarash responded by pawing at me and trying to catch my hand in her mouth.

I started to change my behavior: I chased upright but dropped to all fours during tactical charges. I tried to use all the elements of dog play: the lateral jumps, the quick head tosses to signal running away, the jerky barks, the play bows. It was wonderful to watch Tarash when she was fully immersed in the game, displaying the same vitality, ease, and caprice that I had seen in capering pigs. The difference was that as a participant, I could perceive both her emotions and my own.

Like me, Tarash obviously enjoyed not only her skillful maneuvers but also her failures and misfortunes: missing in attempts to catch my waving hand in her jaws, bumping into the door frame when I made a surprise appearance on the other side. We probably would have looked strange to an outside observer, but we didn't care. We were having fun.

After this experience, I can't watch or recall pig play without having a strong mammalian-insider feeling of how much fun they're having. Playing with Tarash gave me an understanding of what other mammals feel when they play. Whatever else its ultimate function, their play, like ours, is about fun.

FELLOW FEELINGS

Whatever emotions animals may experience, the desire to be unique is probably an exclusively human feeling—if not an especially logical or admirable one. Insistent in its service, we've spent centuries establishing distinctions between "us" and "them," setting ourselves above the rest of the earth's creatures, generally to their detriment and ours.

We've seen by now the fallibility of such assumptions when it comes to strong and obvious feelings: love, fear, anger, joy, and grief. They all appear to be present in a great many animals. But what of the more subtle and intricate secondary emotions—among them empathy, trust, embarrassment, shame, resentment, jealousy, and relief? Many scientists believe these complicated, self-reflective feelings require the participation of the neocortex, the part of the brain that evolved latest and appears to be peculiar to primates (like us) and a few other social mammals. The neocortex is the rational, logical part of the brain.

If it's true that one needs a neocortex to navigate emotional depths, then many animals presumably lack the capability to feel all the things that we do. Even so, there are experts who contend that at least some of the subtle emotions are, in fact, found in creatures outside the charmed circle of the "higher" mammals—in deer and cows and donkeys, for instance, in sharks and even perhaps lizards and snakes.

The verdict is still out. We need more information, both about animals and about neurobiology itself. At the very least, though, we can be sure that for all our lordly cerebral grandeur, the expansive and varicolored emotional world we live in is also a world we share—with our closest evolutionary cousins, to be sure, and perhaps with numerous other creatures as well.

PAGE 158: *The facial expressions of chimpanzees lead many to conclude that they also share some of our emotions.*

OPPOSITE: *Young elephants in Kenya at play, practicing skills that will help them compete and survive as they grow older.*

160

GORDON M. BURGHARDT | *University of Tennessee*

Staying Close

Young iguanas like these tend to stay together— sometimes for extended periods—once they've exited the soil in which their eggs have hatched.

It was a hot May morning in Panama, and I was spending another day watching a bare plot of soil from a small, cramped blind on a tiny islet in Gatun Lake. Several months earlier, about one hundred female iguanas had temporarily migrated to the islet, called Slothia, to lay their eggs. We knew that some time after the start of the wet season the eggs hatched. No one had ever recorded the hatchlings' emergence from the nest holes, and that's what I wanted to do.

And this morning it happened. Among other wondrous things I saw and filmed was some remarkably social behavior at the very outset of iguana life. When the little hatchlings poked their heads out of the emergence holes that they'd opened, they looked around repeatedly and finally exited the holes in small groups. They even emerged from different holes, gathered in groups, and after considerable tongue flicking and even some gentle nipping at one another, left the clearing together. It was soon obvious that the baby iguanas, having no mother present, nonetheless had a strong urge to stay close together. From marking experiments performed later, we found that some groups stayed together for several days or weeks, often moving many meters through the dense, lush vegetation.

Green iguanas, it turns out, are highly social animals throughout their lives, but particularly when young. They actually spend much

163

time in physical contact with one another. At night, many of the hatchlings sleep exposed on low branches in shrubs. I often found two animals sleeping one atop the other. Other times I saw groups of five, seven, or more animals all touching one or two other hatchlings. Apparently, all this togetherness has adaptive value: There's evidence that individuals in such groups may grow faster or have lower predation. Perhaps this is because a predator jarring a branch full of iguanas startles several of them, the signal spreading through adjacent tails and limbs, prompting escape.

After our own observations, Venezuelan researchers Jesus Rivas and Luis Levin made the remarkable discovery that male hatchling green iguanas seem to preferentially put themselves at risk compared to their sisters. If a model of a predatory bird swooped down over a group of hatchling iguanas, the females generally froze, while the males ran forward in a way that could be characterized as luring or distracting the predator. Or, amazingly, the males sometimes jumped on their sisters' backs. In short, males were willing to sacrifice themselves to save their sisters and their sisters' genes. Why should they do this? In evolutionary terms, the behavior may make sense because females breed when younger than males, and almost all adult females lay eggs. Adult males, however, reach maturity much more slowly and only a few large males attract most of the females to their territories. Most males, therefore, sire few offspring, and thus natural selection would favor altruism by young, untested males.

So goes the standard behavioral ecology explanation for the phenomena: Togetherness in young iguanas and altruism in adult males foster survival. This explanation tells us absolutely nothing, though, about the decision making that dictates the behaviors, or about the private experiences accompanying the decisions. Close contact with a group may provide a feeling of security that, as with us, can be pleasurable and relaxing. In the predator-threat situation, males act differently from females and may feel somewhat different emotions.

The question of feeling also arises in iguana mating behavior. It's been shown both in the field and in captivity that when mating season comes around, both males and females have favored partners—and show a distaste for other would-be mates. One male in our lab repeatedly attacked a female, recognizing her even after an absence of about a year. His rejection of her was swift and intense, but what about his response to his favored female companions?

People normally wouldn't think lizards capable of showing pleasure or joy, but when you study a species closely or live with it intimately, it's possible to detect subtle signs of emotion. Does the animal approach or withdraw? Is the heart beating fast? Are the eyes closed even when the animal is awake? Is the tail relaxed, raised, rigid, or thrashing? Is the body raised, flattened, or normal? Has the body color darkened? Is the flap of skin under the neck, called a dewlap, extended or relaxed? All these physical signs may indicate arousal, stress, social acceptance, sexual invitation, or other moods, though we still understand too little about the emotional language of iguanas and other reptiles.

The signs are not that different from comparable signals we use to measure emotional responses in mammals. Ultimately, brain and neurotransmitter information will allow us to determine if the mechanisms underlying the social behaviors of mammals, including primates, are found in lizards as well. I have renewed confidence that they will turn out to be similar every time Emma, our lab mascot iguana, raises her head to be scratched and rubbed. A cat she's not, but she can still be considered affectionate. If a fire broke out in my laboratory, Emma would be the first animal, though far from the most valuable one, that I would try to save.

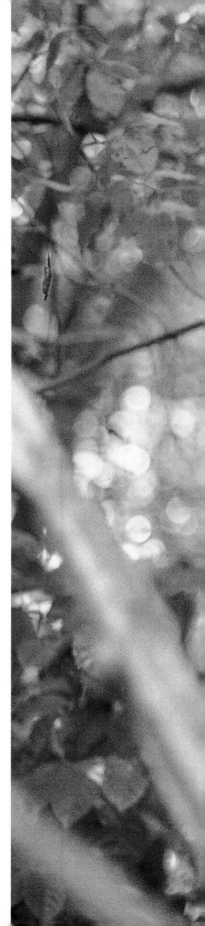

JANE GOODALL | *Explorer-in-residence, National Geographic Society*

Pride Goeth before a Fall

When Fifi's oldest child, Freud, was five and a half years old, his uncle, Fifi's brother Figan, was the alpha male of the chimpanzee community. Freud was always following Figan and spent hours watching him. In other words, he hero-worshipped the big male.

Once, as Fifi was grooming Figan, Freud climbed up the thin stem of a wild plantain. When he reached the leafy crown, he began swaying back and forth, more and more wildly. Had he been a human child, we would have said he was showing off.

Suddenly there was a crack; the stem broke and Freud tumbled, head first, into the long grass. He fell only a short distance and wasn't hurt. He landed close to me, and as his head emerged from the grass, I saw him look over at Figan: Had his uncle noticed? If he had, he paid no heed but went on with his grooming. Freud very, very quietly climbed a different tree and began to feed.

Young chimpanzees frequently amuse themselves with aerial acrobatics among the branches—and they seldom fall.

LUDĚK BARTOŠ | *Research Institute of Animal Production, Prague, Czech Republic*

A Fall from Grace

Dominant red deer stags who lose their antlers before others are sometimes able to retain their social position during periods when the herd's numbers have decreased. This stag, who has already cast his antlers, is threatening the other one.

My colleagues and I at Zehusice in the Czech Republic have been studying social relationships among red deer for some seventeen years. One of the more arresting phenomena we've observed is the way deer cope with humiliation at the hands of their fellows. And there's plenty of humiliation to be seen, especially among males during antler casting—the seasonal, temporary shedding of the antlers. Usually the high-ranked males cast first. Without their lordly rack of tines, they generally lose their status within the hierarchy until others cast as well. This can take days, sometimes weeks.

It's clearly difficult for the temporarily humbled individual to cope with his diminished position. So it was with an alpha stag called Borivoj, who cast his antlers, fell from grace, and became the frequent object of attack by almost all the bachelors in the group. The lone exception was a stag named Blbec. A rather retiring, peace-loving soul, Blbec didn't have too many interactions of any kind with the other deer. He remained respectful of the antlerless Borivoj—a thankless gesture, as it turned out.

Attacked by nearly everybody else, Borivoj took to using Blbec as a sort of whipping deer. After running from every onslaught, Borivoj would look around, spot the placid Blbec, and have at him. However hard he tried to keep his distance or appear nonthreatening, Blbec would have to endure Borijov's furious and high-handed assaults. Finally, fed up, Blbec went off by himself to wait for the group's usual hierarchy to reassert itself.

Another season, the individual who started the antler-casting period was Pista, a big alpha stag. Noting Pista's vulnerability, another stag, Jubinal, began reveling in his short-term superiority. Many times each day he approached Pista, threatening him elaborately and at a distance, so all the other animals would see it. Pista lowered his head and tried to disappear. But even this degradation was insufficient for Jubinal, who followed Pista for minutes at a time, often forcing him away from the rest of the herd. Poor Pista, head dragging, ground his teeth noisily. In this deer species, teeth-grinding usually signifies a threat. In Pista's case, however, it apparently expressed helpless fury.

From our human point of view, it would be understandable if Pista, with antlers and honor restored, had humbled in turn his upstart tormentor. But this was not the case. Our data on antagonistic interactions before, during, and after antler casting (when the former alpha stag became dominant again) showed that Pista attacked Jubinal no more often than he did anyone else. No attempt at vengeance was detected. We might conclude from this, I suppose, that either deer have a short memory, or they're far more forgiving than human males might be if subjected to similar humiliation.

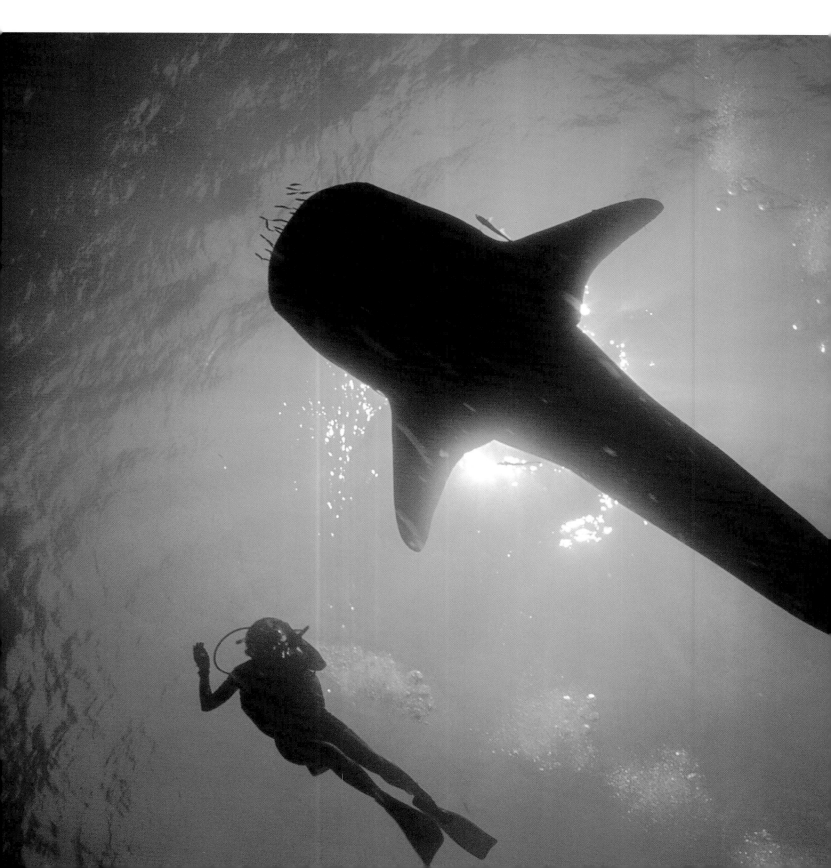

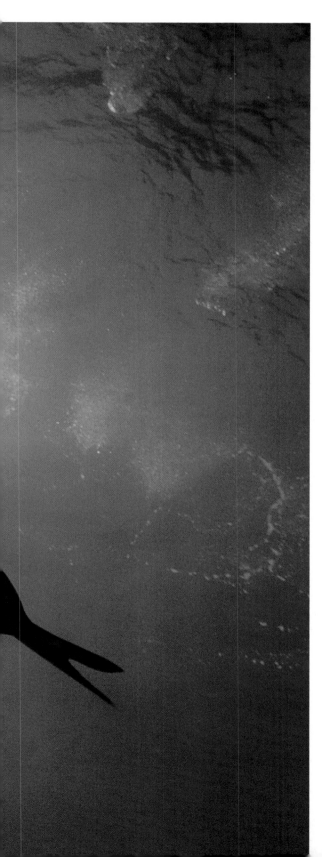

A young whale shark feeds on phytoplankton near the ocean's surface. A decade or so ago, little was known about these great fish, but they're becoming increasingly popular with ecotourists.

MICHAEL TOBIAS | *Los Angeles*

A Gentle Heart

She's the largest fish in the world, a shark by name—half a dozen gills, retractable eyes, cartilage in place of bones—but little else to suggest the traditional shark most normally thought of. Her name, whale shark, derives from her size, but there's no other reason to think of her as a whale. Aside from the fact that her tail moves laterally, while a whale's moves vertically, there are other distinguishing characteristics that signal a profound emotional core to the whale shark that differs by form and degree from that of whales.

The thousands of stories stemming from experiences with whales could fill a library. But all the scientific know-how fails to measure the deep social bonds that flow from encounters in the wild between human and whale—bonds that include trust, love, empathy, poetic rhapsodies, and trysts without beginning or end. These immersions with whales are true enough, and there are many stories about them.

But with sharks, the legacy couldn't be more radically different. From *Jaws* to "Shark Week" on cable television, the image of a man-eater has fueled a universal hatred of the dozens of species of shark, when in fact, there's no such thing as a man-eater; shark attacks are extremely rare, and when they do occur they're usually like a dog biting the leg of an intruder in his yard. It's the teeth, of course, that doom

171

the shark and make it the test of manhood for all those fishermen who've ever bragged about killing it, just as the wolf and the rattlesnake have become victims of their own fangs, the elephant of its tusks. The larger truth is that sharks are no more predatory than butterflies, hummingbirds, or ladybugs.

And yet, for all the tomes churned out about sharks, the whale shark remains elusive and counterintuitive. Most mysterious of all is its inherent emotional capacity. We think of emotion as that ability to be moved, or to move another—to evoke a response that comes from the heart. The whale shark has a gigantic heart and a massive brain. It has put to work a hundred million years of docility toward a purpose, and what might that experience be? The longest experiment in nonviolence ever undertaken in the entire biological history of the planet, by one of its very largest life forms. What does that mean?

The whale shark should become the poster child for all international wildlife conservation and true conscience. There is no gentler creature on Earth.

To this I am a witness. For hours and hours my colleagues and I swam with a dozen whale sharks, including Nachos, the name given him by a local doctor and part-time fisherman, over the course of two days. Swimming with Nachos and his friends, I found myself completely severed from time. I was unsnarled from all connections and became one with Nachos. These sharks came up to us in the water, swam around us and with us, and truly wanted to

make some sort of metaphysical, primal exchange. We swam side by side, entered into trust and fellowship, extended every mutual admiration, displayed all the forces of poetry and passion and delight that can be interpreted according to any free range of the senses.

At one point we were surrounded by three of the sharks, two of whom were floating side by side, grazing the bounty of phytoplankton. Together they constituted sixty thousand pounds of loving flesh, moving at three tandem knots. They were speaking with one another, silently sharing. What feelings did they have? I'm certain that between them, at the heart of their ancient relationship, was the very essence of bliss as the poets and saints have always thought of it. A joy that we spend our lives aspiring to. An integrity that has no conflict. They aren't sabotaging themselves, or acting out conflicts between their conscious and subconscious selves. Nor are they solitary. They move frequently together, inches apart, and it's clear to the observer that they deeply love and are committed to one another.

I told the sharks, "I love you," and they seemed to reply in kind. A gentleness that surpasseth science. Their size dictates their confidence. In a hundred million years, no other creature has ever systematically preyed upon them. They're as big as a five-story building; their compassion and purity a skyscraper of living dreams, bigger still.

I came away emotionally in shock. I have swum with thousands of other fish species on every continent but have never been so reshaped in my imagination by another creature. Nachos and his friends transformed, transfixed, and

reformed my nature, and it happened within minutes of being in their presence. I cannot account for the mystery, nor would I ever presume or recommend its translation.

We need mystery. We need sharks. We need to be reminded of our petite nature before the massive truth of the seas that cover most of this planet. Absent such modesty, we will continue to assault the oceans with our own tools of predation. The passions of the whale shark move me to tears, to joy, to prayer. They are on the planet as messengers, embodiments of the best the world has to offer.

I come back to their emotional lives. These sharks exhibit bliss, the ultimate state of meditation and indwelling referred to by such diverse luminaries as Buddha and Thoreau: the immanence that the history of spirituality and art, whether in the writings of Saint Francis and Swedenborg or the canvasses of Vermeer or van Gogh, have advocated.

Nachos lives in what the Australian aborigines call the dreamtime. And that's the place to which I was plunged when I encountered Nachos. That he wanted something from me—a sign of contact—suggests that his great mind swirls with curiosity and imagination, a desire that more than hints at the fact that his heart, his tens of thousands of pounds of flesh, muscle, and cold blood, are filled with emotions.

No other creature occupies so enormous a niche with so few demands. That suggests a modesty consistent with extraordinarily sophisticated thought and sensibility. To attribute deep emotions to a shark is a fitting approach to the twenty-first century, a way to partake of its humility and become the better for it.

SUE SAVAGE-RUMBAUGH | *Georgia State University*

Sibling Rivalry

Have you ever been jealous of the accomplishments of your siblings? Kanzi is. For a long time he was the only "star" bonobo, a pygmy chimpanzee, at the Language Research Center in Atlanta. When film crews came to visit, they weren't interested in his younger sister Panbanisha; they wanted to film only him.

Kanzi could use a keyboard, blow up balloons, solve complicated mazes and puzzles on a computer with a joystick, make stone tools, and understand really difficult sentences. Moreover, he had stage presence and charisma. And he loved to play to the camera: When he awoke one morning after a two-week filming session to find the crew had gone, he was so upset that he refused to leave his bedroom. If there was no one to applaud his accomplishments, why bother? Then there was the time the photographer came to take his picture when Kanzi was sick with the flu. The show must go on. The bonobo wiped the drainage from his nose; cleared his chest; assumed his erect, seated, head-high, profile pose; and held it while his picture was snapped. Afterward, Kanzi collapsed again into the fever.

In time, though, his younger sister Panbanisha began to provide a little competition. The *London Times* was interested in getting pictures of her. Kanzi waited patiently while the photographer snapped away, calling that he was available as well. We told him to wait his turn, that he would be next. But then the *Times* people decided they didn't want Kanzi's picture after all. He was devastated. That night he bit two long grooves in his electronic keyboard, rendering it useless.

He also began to be very jealous of anything Panbanisha did well or got compliments for. When she tried to make stone tools, he bristled. As her chipping sounds increased and it began to seem she was hitting the rocks in just the right way, with just the right noise—the kind that precedes the creation of a suitably large flake—Kanzi displayed at her. (A simian display is a stylized, quadrupedal rushing that can end in a body slam if you don't get out of the way.) She dropped the stones. When it became obvious that she was coloring many pictures in her coloring book and writing some lexigrams, or symbols, clearly on the floor—better than he could—he scattered her crayons.

The next time Panbanisha started to make a tool, she just hit the rocks lightly together and looked at Kanzi with an appealingly pitiable "I can't do it" expression. His male superiority thus affirmed, Kanzi gracefully deigned to make a tool for her and hand it over. Panbanisha was shrewd enough not only to make a tool but to know when it was better not to make a

Happily the center of the attention, Kanzi displays his computer skills for the camera. The pygmy chimpanzee's smile is apt to vanish, however, when his younger sister shows off her own talents.

tool and to feign incompetence, allowing her brother to share the fruits of his labor while maintaining his self-image.

Then it came time to try and play the new electric guitar. Panbanisha and Kanzi had both tried once before, and it was clear that she was better at it. As soon as the new guitar was mentioned again, Kanzi began to display at Panbanisha again; he didn't even want her in the room. So I took her outdoors, leaving Kanzi behind. He screamed and pleaded to go, but we ignored him. Finally, in a fit of pique, he grabbed a toy panda bear and tore off its arms. Then he felt ashamed and tried to put them back. When he couldn't, he carried them around and around the room, keeping his head down and not look-

ing anyone in the eye. He elected to punish himself by staying in the tool room while Panbanisha returned and played her music.

Kanzi, being part bonobo and part human in his cultural heritage, vacillates between the undisciplined id and sensitive ego—one minute aggressive and bullying, the next reflective and hurt. Sometimes the switch is so complete and so rapid that it's difficult to grasp what's happening. Kanzi is pure feeling, all feeling, straight from the heart, and the expression of those feelings—jealousy among them—is strong and unadulterated every time.

175

MICHAEL W. FOX | *The Humane Society of the United States*

The Nature of Compassion

Michael Fox is at the center of what he calls a "love pyramid," formed by rescued dogs given sanctuary at the India Project for Animals and Nature (IPAN) at the Hill View Farm Animal Refuge, south India.

As a veterinarian and an ethologist, I've been fortunate to see animals in a variety of situations over the years. They've been my teachers. Dogs and wolves in particular have taught me that they share with we humans the ability to empathize—to feel what others are feeling. Empathy underlies altruistic behavior and acts of heroism, as we see in dogs and other animals that have rescued drowning children and saved human companions from burning homes.

Empathy is most evident in parent animals responding to the needs of offspring. The parents, especially nursing females, may be sensitized by hormonal changes, but the source of their behavior in no way diminishes its tenderness—a love not necessarily limited to their own young. I knew an Irish setter who lived on a farm and occasionally brought home baby rabbits she'd killed. But when she had a false pregnancy, she brought the young rabbits home live and protected them.

During parent-infant interactions, as between a wolf and her cubs, signals sent through facial expressions, various tail and body postures, and vocalizations from the cubs evoke predictable caregiving responses from the mother. Body signals, distress calls (cries, yelps, whimpers), and sounds of contentment (sighs, groans, grunts, purrs) are common to many species. They probably account not only for

altruism within a species but among different species: The cries of a puppy in distress touch most human hearts, moving us to help it; similarly, a kitten's cries make some dogs respond with tender care, gently licking and comforting the little creature.

Part of empathy comes from self-care and self-comfort being extended to others. Dogs and other animals take care of their body surfaces, groom themselves, and seek to maintain physical comfort and emotional security; and when they can, they often offer this care to others. One of my most poignant early experiences of empathy was witnessing a street dog in Kashmir, India, licking the sores on his emaciated mate and snapping at the flies around her face. When I gave them food, he let her eat first.

Every day at India Project for Animals and Nature's (IPAN) animal refuge in southern India, operated by my wife, Deanna Krantz, I saw interspecies altruism and empathy: cattle grooming ponies, dogs grooming goats, horses grooming buffaloes. Such nurturing promotes more than mere cleanliness: During grooming and stroking, the object's heart rate drops dramatically, part of a relaxation response that's physiologically and psychologically beneficial.

Of the two hundred animals at IPAN's animal refuge, the adult dogs, cows, and donkeys showed the most empathy. Certain individuals, irrespective of age and sex, were more empathic caregivers than others. Two dogs in particular always lay down protectively beside a newborn foal or calf, or by an animal recovering from surgery.

In my book *The Soul of the Wolf,* I alluded to the notion that members of the wolf pack are of one mind, socially and emotionally connected. I believe, in fact, that many species, including our own, are so attuned, joined with one another through the empathosphere, a universal realm of feeling that can transcend both space and time. It enables animals to engage in extrasensory perception, a remote sensing that allows them to locate over distance those with whom they have an emotional bond and possibly to feel what they're feeling.

From more than thirty years of writing a syndicated newspaper column, I've learned much about the empathic powers of our animal companions. Many readers have told me how their dogs and cats know when another family member has died at a hospital. One reader reported on a poodle that became frantic in the house at around the time the family's eldest son was seriously injured in a car accident. Then there was the Siamese cat who began to cry in

distress at exactly the time his German shepherd companion died on the operating table at the veterinary hospital.

The most remarkable news clipping was sent by a reader hwo received it from a relative in Australia some ten years ago. It recounted how a dog saved her master's life by bringing him water when he was crippled by a stroke. The elderly man had lain paralyzed in bed for nine days before he was found. During this time, his six-year-old sheepdog had soaked towels in her drinking bowl or the toilet and carried them to him so he could suck the water.

Through the empathosphere, I've had some vivid experiences during telephone communications involving animals. Sometimes I can visualize the animal's condition and feel it in my own body. Like other veterinarians, I often feel something in my body while examining an animal patient, the power of empathy being, I believe, part of the healing art. Some people have speculated that certain animals not only take on the personalities of their human companions but also some of their emotional and physical ailments. This again may be because they are so empathic, engaged in a sympathetic resonance with their loved ones.

Metaphysical speculations aside, one of the most empathic animals I've ever known was Tanza, a street dog my wife brought back from Tanzania. Tanza would show great concern when any child fell down or cried, or when a family member got sick or had to wear a bandage or an eye patch. She once even performed minor surgery on her companion dog Lizzie, whom she regularly groomed, fastidiously snipping off the whiskers on her muzzle. One evening I found four warts under Lizzie's lower lip. I showed them to Tanza, thinking I should excise them the next day. But Tanza was clearly concerned and licked the warts as Lizzie stood quite still. The next morning Lizzie's warts were all gone. Tanza had licked and nibbled them all away without causing any bleeding or damage.

Lizzie likes to bring a gift whenever anyone she knows comes to the house, grabbing the first thing available, usually a ball or a bone. Once, desperately searching for something with which to greet an old friend on the front porch, she came forward with a large leaf in her mouth, which the man graciously accepted.

Tanza, Lizzie, and my many other animal friends have taught me that humans are not the only creatures who desire comfort, security, and love, who want freedom from pain, loneliness, fear, and sadness, and who've evolved empathy. Animals show us every day that they have feelings for us and for one another—feelings that should move us all to respect their rights and interests and to treat them with compassion and understanding.

Frans B. M. de Waal | *Yerkes Regional Primate Research Center, Atlanta*

Making Up with a Kiss

After conflict, reconciliation among chimpanzees takes a very human, mouth-to-mouth form. The kiss here is bestowed by a female (right) on the alpha male of a colony at the Yerkes Regional Primate Research Center in Atlanta.

About twenty-five years ago at a zoo in Arnhem, Netherlands, a dramatic sequence unfolded before my eyes. A large chimpanzee colony was locked indoors in one of its winter halls. Right after the highest-ranking male finished a charging display, in which he swaggered about with hair standing on end, he attacked a female. This caused great commotion as other apes came to her defense. After the group had calmed down, an unusual silence followed, as if the apes were waiting for something to happen. Then, after a couple of minutes, the entire colony suddenly burst out hooting, and one of the males produced rhythmic noise on metal drums stacked in the corner of the hall. In the midst of this pandemonium, two chimpanzees kissed and embraced.

I reflected on the scene for several hours before the term "reconciliation" came to mind. This was after I realized that the two embracing individuals had been the same male and female who were in the original fight. Since that day, I've followed the peace-making behavior of chimpanzees and other primates, or as we call it nowadays, their "conflict resolution." Others have found the same behavior in a great variety of species, including primates in the wild and nonprimates such as dolphins, hyenas, and goats.

It seems that many social animals know how to reconcile, and for good reason. Though conflict among them is inevitable, animals must often depend on one another. They forage for food together, warn one another of predators, and stand united to defend territory. They need to maintain good relationships despite occasional flare-ups, not unlike married couples.

The definition of a reconciliation (a friendly reunion between opponents not long after a fight) is straightforward, but the emotions involved are hard to pinpoint. The least that occurs—though this alone is remarkable—is that negative emotions such as aggression and fear are overcome in order to move to a positive interaction like a kiss.

Primates have different ways of reconciling, from the buttocks-holding rituals of stumptail macaques to erotic contacts among bonobos. In all cases, though, the behavior looks intensely positive. Since we ourselves experience the switch from hostility to attraction as "forgiveness," we may speculate that even though forgiveness is sometimes construed as an exclusively human achievement, it's an ancient pattern born of social necessity.

Another possible factor in reconciliation is concern about the relationship. Primates form close and much-valued friendships, expressed in grooming and traveling together. Friends defend each other against aggressors and are willing to take risks on each other's behalf. This is why fights often create anxiety—the worry that a good relationship will deteriorate or end. In the Arnhem colony, two males, Nikkie and Yeroen, occasionally fought, even though at other times they supported each other, groomed together, and dominated the colony as a team. Nikkie was the alpha male,

An adult male chimpanzee at the Yerkes Center is embraced by a young friend. The older chimpanzee is screaming, having just lost a fight, and the juvenile is offering him consolation and reassurance.

and each time he got into a quarrel with his older ally, Yeroen, his position became shaky; he couldn't on his own keep a third male, Luit, under control.

We easily identify with Nikkie's dilemma, a typically political one: wanting to win the fight with Yeroen while at the same time not alienating him. Most of the time, Nikkie gave in or quickly reconciled in order to stay on good terms with his ally.

The anxiety involved in such situations is measurable. Just like college students who scratch their heads when faced with a tough exam question, self-scratching indicates anxiety in other primates. My co-worker, Filippo Aureli, conducted studies that measured scratching after fights. He found that recent victims of aggression scratch themselves at high rates but that they stop after a reconciliation. This suggests that reunion with the opponent has a calming effect. Aureli also found that the aggressors scratch themselves too, especially after fights with their closest friends and kin. This means that fights induce anxiety not only about continued aggression—in which case only losers should seem anxious—but also about the state of the relationship.

People with young apes living in their home have told me of the surprising intensity of the animals' desire to make up after being reprimanded. After a while, the ape would jump into its chastiser's lap, giving a tight hug and then a sigh of relief. The fear of losing a loved partner is one of the deepest we can experience, and I'm convinced we share it with the other social animals.

ELIZABETH MARSHALL THOMAS | *New Hampshire*

A Friend in Need

A good shepherd looks out for the animals in his care. Part–German shepherd Ruby seems to understand this as she tends her little shih tzu friend, Wicket.

One day in early spring I went on an outing in the woods near my New Hampshire home with a friend, his eight-year-old son, and four dogs: my friend's shih tzu, Wicket, my shepherd-cross, Ruby, and my two Australian cattle dogs. The friend and his boy rode an all-terrain vehicle, and the dogs and I walked.

We crossed a partly frozen stream—all but Wicket, who was too small. His owners barreled onward, unaware of the shih tzu's plight. The poor little dog was getting frightened at being left behind, out in the woods, far from home. I was watching to see if he'd brave the icy water and was about to go back for him, when my Ruby went to the rescue instead.

She went back across the stream and greeted Wicket. He was extremely glad to see her, and jumped on her as he would on a person. She then tried to lead him across. He eagerly followed her right up to the water's edge but at the last minute he stopped. Ruby went back to him and tried a second, then a third time to lead him. No luck. Getting a new idea, she ran along the bank until she came to a place where the stream was narrow. Here, instead of wading, she jumped across. Wicket followed her to the narrow place, but he didn't dare jump. So

Ruby then returned to the regular crossing place and tried again and again, perhaps seven or eight times, and, although the people and the other dogs were by this time very far away, Ruby would not abandon Wicket. After perhaps ten unsuccessful attempts, she at last persuaded him to follow her across. Then, with Wicket at her heels, Ruby ran on to catch up with the ATV. Afterwards, until we came out of the woods, Wicket stayed with Ruby, whether she was near his owners or not.

I was moved by this because Ruby is a very humble dog, low on our totem pole, and so is Wicket. Quietly, all on her own, with no aid from people, she helped the little guy.

Benjamin B. Beck | *National Zoological Park, Smithsonian Institution*

A Violation of Trust

Perhaps because it's so bright, the hamadryas baboon was regarded in ancient Egypt as sacred to Thoth, the god of learning and writing. As do other baboons, they communicate through vocal calls, postures, and tail signals.

In the early 1970s, I observed a four-year-old female hamadryas baboon (*Papio hamadryas*) at the Brookfield Zoo forge a unique, cooperative relationship with her older brother—one that had unexpected results.

The male, whom we called Peewee, had learned to use a long rod as a tool to get choice food that was placed out of reach in front of his cage. But then we put the tool in an adjacent cage, one that held several of his family members but that he himself was too big to enter. There were two ways for Peewee to get the rod. He could (and did) reach through the connecting door and snatch it when one of the group members brought it close enough. Or, because the female, Pat, and the rest of the family were small enough to pass through the door, he could wait for one of them to bring the tool into his cage. I thought it unlikely that the second event would ever happen, since monkeys had never been observed using tools cooperatively (apes had, on a few occasions.)

On the first four trials of this experiment, Peewee snatched the rod, used it to get the food, and ate most of it, allowing others only scattered bits of the least desired items. When he tried to snatch the tool, the others resisted and screamed. On the fifth trial, however, Pat suddenly and directly got the rod and intentionally brought it to Peewee. There was no snatching (even when the tool was in reach of his cage), no screaming, and no resistance. He used the rod to get the food, and he and Pat each ate about half of it.

Pat and Peewee quickly refined their cooperative relationship, but her share of the food dwindled. Soon she was getting only about 15 percent. Sometimes she sat next to Peewee as he ate, staring into his face from inches away. Sometimes she simply paced agitatedly around the cage as he dined on his outsized share. Sometimes she surreptitiously placed her hand over a scattered tidbit without looking at it and ate it later when Peewee was distracted. But because of male dominance she never dared take a choice bit directly, so she got mostly leftovers. My interpretation was that Pat was growing resentful but could not express outright anger or aggression toward a male baboon who was twice her size, had dagger-like canines, and was clearly dominant.

One day, as Peewee ate and Pat paced, she passed by the door that joined the two cages just as another family member suddenly stuck its head through. Startled, Pat screamed involuntary. Peewee leaped to the door, threw Pat out of the way, and began threatening the baboons in the other cage. By chance, however, Pat had landed in the middle of the food pile, and she quickly stuffed her cheek pouches.

On their very next cooperative venture, after Pat had brought the tool and Peewee had used it to get and monopolize the food, she went directly to the door between the cages and screamed. There was no other group member on the other side, but again Peewee leaped to the door, pushing Pat aside. She ran directly to the food and again stuffed her pouches.

This maneuver was repeated two or three times before Peewee invented a counterstrategy: He would pull the food pile across the cage floor in his encircling arms and then sit in the door while he ate. Pat's successful but short-lived strategy for dealing with her resentment of Peewee was foiled.

She continued to make do with her paltry 15 percent share of the food, except for certain occasions: When she was ovulating and presented to and copulated willingly with Peewee, he allowed her a larger portion. Though I don't think she intentionally manipulated him through sex, I do feel that he was intentionally leaving food for her on these days.

I published the exciting cooperative tool use result in *Science*, but I've never before written about the full tale of greed and deceit. Many animals get angry and even resentful when they don't get what they desire. But Pat's was an especially deep resentment, one based on a violation of trust.

BERND WÜRSIG | *Texas A&M University*

In a Party Mood

Swimming with friends, a dusky dolphin executes a somersault. Of the forty or so species of dolphins, duskies are among the most acrobatic. Their leaps are sometimes associated with socializing and play, but they may also be chased out of the water by other dolphins.

When dusky dolphins (*Lagenorhynchus obscurus*) herd or corral schooling fishes, they can't easily be bothered. An approaching vessel elicits no reaction, nor does even a human swimmer in the water. They swim past you as though you weren't there. You feel ignored. Aren't dolphins supposed to ride the bow wave and cavort around you?

But when dolphins—all dolphins—haven't fed for several days, they get downright ornery. Not only will they not approach, but they'll deliberately swim away. If you persist, they'll dive under the boat and surface far behind it in an obvious attempt to evade the intrusion. A dolphin group of several dozen can easily lose humans with these ploys. They're hungry and searching for food, and they make it quite clear that they don't want company. The human mood called "surliness" comes to mind.

But after a successful bout of feeding, the mood quickly changes. The dolphins that evaded you in the morning and ignored you half an hour ago are now eager to rush to the bow, whistle loudly, leap, and circle under and around you. They're in a party mood, and their willingness to interact with humans (and other species) is a natural outgrowth of a high level of sociability. Their playfulness may even be important in reinforcing their social

189

bonds: "Let's play together, and we'll be able to work together more efficiently as well."

Much sexual activity goes on during the spirited dolphin parties, and it's unclear how much is for procreation, for social signaling, or just for fun. There seems to be general joy or happiness (and considerable sexual aggression) in the after-feeding party. Dolphins travel and interact most often in dyads and triads at such times—perhaps not unlike humans chatting in small groups at the office party.

What's this? A dolphin is alone, swimming in lazy circles through the party hubbub. This lone animal is likely to be found interacting with something—with a bit of kelp or piece of wood, perhaps. Play is important at this time, and if a dolphin has no partner, it takes up with something else in the environment—jostling it, pushing it, buzzing it with echolocation clicks, investigating with snout or flippers.

If the environmental toy is another living thing, so much the better. In Patagonia, where dusky dolphins herd schooling anchovies toward the surface, marine birds take advantage of this abundant prey to gorge themselves. They then sit on the water, digesting, at precisely the time of the dolphins' after-feeding bash. Dolphins like to play with objects on the water's surface, and what could be more enticing than a pair of skinny, bright orange or pink legs dangling from a feathered, round rump?

I've often seen a lone dusky dolphin approach such a pair of appendages, generally belonging to a kelp gull, slow its speed to almost nothing, open its tooth-lined jaws gingerly (so as not to disturb the oblivious bird above), and gently but firmly close its jaws around one or both legs. Then, surging forward with a sideways toss of the torso, the dolphin pulls the hapless avian beneath the waves. The surprised bird flutters and kicks, the dolphin releases its grip, and the bird bobs to the surface for a frenzy of preening before it flaps off. It's unhurt, save perhaps for its pride.

Oh, if dolphins could only twist their rigid faces into a real smile, for I know they're smiling in their minds at such times: "I got another one just now!" We might call this form of play teasing, or mischievous behavior. Such a sense of fun may not denote an emotion per se, but perhaps it does help reveal a bit about a very intelligent creature who uses its world for more than food, shelter, and procreation.

RICHARD W. BYRNE | *University of St. Andrews, Scotland*

A Sign of Acceptance

Silverback gorilla Ziz insisted on sitting at Jennifer Byrne's feet while he ate his plant, something he had never done before. There were many other plants available, which he had to pass in order to reach Jennifer.

My wife, Jen, and I had been working with the mountain gorillas of Karisoke in Rwanda for only two weeks when an experience began that was unlike anything we'd encountered while working with chimpanzees and baboons in other parts of Africa.

Researcher Pascale Sicotte, whom the gorillas already knew well, had originally introduced us to the long-lasting social unit of gorillas called Group 5, and we seemed immediately to be accepted. As we arrived each morning, the leading silverback, Ziz, looked at us and then typically paid us no further attention, although on a few occasions he strutted unnecessarily close to us or tore at vegetation or branches as he passed. Ziz's slight caution with us seemed only appropriate for a male leading a large group. On the whole, we concluded, we'd never in our field work met with primates so perfectly accustomed to the unobtrusive presence of scientists.

After several hours of recording data on July 29, 1989, Jen and I were standing about five yards apart on a small hill some twenty yards from the nearest gorilla when I noticed Ziz walking toward me, rapidly and directly.

My first concern was that we might unwittingly be standing in the middle of some aggressive encounter, but I could detect no gorillas behind us. Ziz walked straight up to me, then half-turned and sat facing away from me, eating a thistle growing there. He was partly sitting on my feet, and his back was against my legs. The thistle seemed no different from any of the other large thistles on the slope he had crossed to reach me. After two minutes, and with the thistle not fully eaten, he got up and walked over to Jen, repeating the exact same sequence: sitting with his back against her legs, preparing a plant to eat. While he was doing so, a young gorilla playing in a distant tree broke a branch with a sharp crack, and Jen felt a sudden jerk in Ziz's body, suggesting tension. After two or three minutes, Ziz got up and returned to sit touching me, just as before, halfheartedly munching his plant. At last he stood and walked away from us, never looking back.

Astonished by his behavior, we discussed what it might mean. We wondered if, unlikely as it might seem, his actions could be intentional communication of some kind. The more cautious hypothesis—that he came near us because that's where the food was—was implausible: In the lush vegetation of that area, he need not have approached us in order to eat. His behavior, then, appeared to be directed at showing us something important—perhaps that we were in some way accepted.

If so, we reasoned, we could predict that his actions toward us would change from that date. The prediction was confirmed. On no future occasion did Ziz make any of the mildly aggressive displays that he had made during our earlier acquaintance. Moreover, when we arrived at the gorilla group each day thereafter, talking, he didn't bother to turn around and look at us. In fact, he usually didn't even glance up; it was as though he took it for granted that we belonged there, that we constituted no threat.

Such a level of acceptance was something quite unexpected for us. Ziz's new manner didn't appear gradually, as we'd come to expect with normal habituation, but as a sharp change from that day onward. We concluded that his strange and never-repeated actions that July day were meant to convey a message, something like, "OK, now I trust you."

Michel Cabanac | *Laval University, Québec*

In a Fever

Cold-blooded or not, this crocodile is a model of parental concern as the adult ferries a baby in its mouth. Crocodilians (crocodiles, caimans, and alligators) are caring and protective parents.

There are all sorts of emotions we might ascribe to animals just from watching them. But there are also physiological signs—measurable bodily reactions—that can tell us something about creatures' feelings, including the emotions of animals very different from us. Much can be learned, for instance, from observing changes in an animal's temperature.

In the 1960s, scientists recognized that behavior is the most effective way for an animal to maintain its body temperature. Studies showed that once a species develops the ability to move, it will move toward or away from a heat source to stay within a given range of temperatures, called its thermopreferendum. It was also found that the thermopreferendum shifts upward during a viral or bacterial infection. Birds and mammals are warm-blooded and thus theoretically need not move toward an external heat source to keep within their proper temperature range. Even so, they seek out warmer environments when they're feverish. The same behavior applies for cold-blooded creatures—fish, amphibians, and reptiles—that must move toward an external heat source to regulate temperature. By studying how cold-blooded animals respond to fever, it was eventually learned that roundworms, scorpions, insects, crustaceans—all invertebrates, in fact, above the mollusc and flatworm classes—display feverish behaviors after they're injected with fever-

195

producing substances such as bacteria or viruses. In other words, they seek out heat.

Then, in 1970, my friend Edouard Briese and his colleague Maria de Quijada, working at the University of Merida in Venezuela, discovered that mere friendly handling of laboratory rats was enough to make the animals' body temperature rise. Significantly, however, the fever faded with repeated handling, suggesting that the rats got used to the human contact and no longer responded to it thermally. This suggested that the fever was not simply a physiological reflex but seemed dependent on the rat's familiarity with the handler. The fever apparently was, at least in part, an emotional response. And emotion implies cognition—conscious thought—on the animal's part.

Mammals display many physiological signs that we humans can easily identify as similar to what we ourselves experience during emotion; among them are the constriction of blood vessels in the skin, increased heart rate, and pilo-erection—the proverbial "hair standing on end." But emotional fever was a new and interesting finding because it was an invisible response, different from the obvious physiological signals that can communicate alarm or arousal, the signs that are useful for intimidating competition, for instance, or warding off aggressors. So we might call the fever a more "pure" sign of emotion.

Scientists would feel more comfortable, however, if there were other signs of emotions accompanying the fever, and, in fact, there is one: tachycardia, an unusually rapid heart rate.

Mammals that become feverish after being handled also become tachycardic during handling.

If we accept emotional fever and tachycardia as signs of emotion in mammals, then we can use them to detect emotion in other animals. So thinking, we set out to investigate all animals that respond with fever to infection and disease and that also have a nervous system outside the heart to control their heart rate. All vertebrates meet these two criteria. Would they respond to a minor stress, such as gentle handling, as the rats did? We found that birds reacted to handling with tachycardia and emotional fever, as did lizards and tortoises. Fish and frogs, on the other hand, exhibited no fever or tachycardia when they were handled. Absence of any sign of emotion may be taken as an indication that fish and amphibians are not "conscious" animals and behave mostly like robots.

If mammals, birds, and reptiles experience emotion, they are conscious. The next question is: Do they feel sensory pleasure? One way to find out is to place the animal in a situation where it need not to do anything but is offered a useless, though presumably pleasurable, sensory experience. Rats will go into a deadly cold for the pleasure of reaching a palatable bait, even though regular chow is available in their warm nest. Therefore, they know pleasure. The option of braving the cold is open to them because they can shiver to regulate their temperature. Lizards, however, cannot shiver. Faced with entering a cold environment to feed themselves, they venture out for as long and often as their survival permits. But if less-appealing food is available in a warm environment, they refuse to go into the cold for the palatable bait. They

These young iguanas appear to be enjoying a companionable family moment. Although science has not been able to determine what they feel, there is evidence that they experience sensory pleasure.

"prefer" to feed on chow and renounce the pleasure of the bait that carries with it the displeasure of the cold. The same type of experiment on humans yields similar results, which can be described as a tendency by human subjects to maximize their sensory pleasure. Therefore, lizards very likely experience sensory pleasure.

The tentative conclusion that reptiles have consciousness and amphibians do not can be attacked from two opposing sides. On the one hand, it may be argued that the signs displayed by mammals, birds, and reptiles are in no way proof that they experience emotion and that consciousness is a prerogative of the human brain. True. These signs are not proof that the animal thinks and possesses a mental experience, but after all, what proof do we have that other humans also think and possess a mental experience? They tell us they do, but language too is a behavior—an indirect sign of the mental experience taking place within. On the other hand, it may be argued that the absence of fever and cardiac response in amphibians and fish in no way proves that they do not experience emotion when handled and that lower animals also may be conscious. Also true.

But of course, both arguments cannot be true at the same time—and there the matter stands. Until new evidence makes a firmer conclusion possible, we may accept that the truth lies somewhere in between, and that consciousness emerged in the ancestors of present-day reptiles.

Andrew Whiten | *University of St. Andrews, Scotland*

Walking in Another's Shoes

Charting the emotional landscape of other animals is one scientific task we can set ourselves. But a step beyond lies another fascinating question: How do animals perceive one another's emotions? Do they merely react to what's on the surface, or might they instead see deeper, assessing the feelings of others as states of mind comparable to their own? When we humans do this, we call it empathy. Are animals ever empathic? Are they capable of putting themselves in another's shoes?

I once watched as Mercury, a young male chimpanzee, approached a hollow tube in search of food, only to jump back startled by what he'd discovered. I was less surprised than he, since I had put the surprise—an iguana—there for him to find. It was part of an experiment designed to study the social understanding of chimpanzees. What happened next, as Mercury's mother came to see what the fuss was about, will bring us to the subject of empathy; but first I need to explain the experiment.

Like many similar ones, it was designed to answer questions raised by observations of primates in the wild. My colleague Richard Byrne and I had noted that wild baboons we'd studied appeared quite naturally to "tune in" to what their groupmates appeared interested in—a kind of empathy in itself, perhaps. Collating all the information collected by ourselves and others, we kept finding signs that primates were very good at both monitoring and manipulating what their companions were doing. In the wild, however, it's difficult to be sure of that. Measuring just how well an animal can get inside another's head demands the kind of experiment in which Mercury, a chimpanzee living in a small captive group at Georgia State University's field station, was involved.

Near a corner of the chimpanzees' large enclosure, I'd arranged several large tubes, situated so they'd all be visible to a chimp positioned in the corner. One chimp or another from Mercury's group checked the tubes for food scraps each morning. On just such an occasion, Mercury discovered the iguana, a stimulus that didn't terrify him but did make him jump back, utter a few alarm calls, and then stare intently down the tube housing the lizard. As he moved away, the experimental question was about to be answered: Since the pipes were all quite close together, had the other chimps read Mercury's attention focus well enough to know which pipe to approach and cautiously explore?

One by one, they checked out the right pipe. Confirmation was logged scientifically

Finding an iguana in a pipe in his home enclosure (left), chimpanzee Mercury signals alarm. (Well, wouldn't you?) At right, he watches as his mother moves in cautiously to investigate.

about how well chimpanzees could home in on exactly what foci in the environment were preoccupying their companions. But I'm first and foremost an ethologist, and I looked for more: Amid the rigor of such experimentation, it's often the unplanned, spontaneous actions of my subjects that capture my attention, suggesting there's something complex happening beyond the experiment's tidy parameters.

On this occasion, the unexpected happened as Mercury's aging mother, Lana, found herself inexorably, if cautiously, drawn to the pipes. Clearly she'd read both the emotional significance and attentional focus of her son well, and she gingerly angled to peer down the pipe where the iguana lurked. What fascinated me, however, was Mercury's reaction. As his mother inched carefully forward, so did he. Then, just at the point at which Lana would first spot the iguana, Mercury, who had been quiet for several minutes while raptly monitoring his mother's approach, let out a loud new yap of alarm.

The timing was so precise that it struck me that the chimp was empathizing with his

mother as she approached the lizard. Perhaps Mercury was sufficiently able to put himself into her position to guess the instant when she'd see it, so his motivation to warn her was rekindled. Or, if he were really putting himself in her shoes, he may have felt her alarm himself and yapped in response. In either case, Mercury would have shown an emotional attunement with his mother's perspective on the world— a prospect with far-reaching consequences if it truly reflects chimpanzees' social perceptions.

This is but a single observation—not a basis for firmly concluding how chimps read others' emotion. On the other hand, perhaps it offers just the kind of insight we'd best not ignore if we want our more systematic research to probe deeper into animal psyches.

MARC HAUSER | *Harvard University*

If Monkeys Could Blush

Secure, at least for the moment, in his lordly masculinity, a rhesus monkey accepts grooming from a female.

Cayo Santiago is a beautiful Caribbean island off the coast of Puerto Rico. Since 1938, it's been home to several hundred rhesus monkeys. For the past decade I've been studying them, focusing on their vocal behavior and cognitive abilities. The process has been facilitated by the fact that dozens of researchers have visited the island, rendering the monkeys quite used to humans. In general, they treat us like moving trees. As long as we keep our distance, they engage in normal social behavior and ignore us.

In 1992, I was studying rhesus monkey mating behavior. My goal was to try and understand why males make loud, individually distinctive vocalizations while they're copulating. Since not all males call, the problem was to figure out the costs and benefits of calling as opposed to remaining silent. To address this problem, I selected several males and each day followed one individual from dawn to dusk.

During the mating season, which lasts for about four months, some males form exclusive liaisons with sexually receptive females while other males float, trying to mate whenever they can. In either case, rhesus males typically copulate several times within a period of fifteen minutes or so, stop for a while, and then resume another copulatory bout. The session often ends when the male ejaculates.

One day I was following an individual designated A74, an alpha male who was in consort with a middle-ranking female, F38. I watched several bouts of mating, each ending before A74 had ejaculated. F38 seemed distracted and often moved away before A74 could finish. Toward the end of the day, F38 appeared at last to be more relaxed, and apparently as a result, A74 was able to complete a copulation bout to his satisfaction. After he'd ejaculated, he dismounted. With head held high and eyes gazing upward, he walked off, stiff-legged and confident, as if thinking, "Damn, I'm good." Not more than ten feet away from F38, he marched straight into a ditch that he'd failed to notice. He tumbled and landed heavily on his side. Quickly he scanned the scene. Was anyone watching? Apparently no one else was around, and his consort was looking in the opposite direction. A74 quickly picked himself up, ran over to F38, and stood there, back arched, head held high, and tail up, waiting to be groomed. To me he looked prototypically alpha, a male brimming with confidence.

But what had A74 felt like when he landed in the ditch? Male readers of this story almost certainly will recall that feeling of embarrassment one gets when an attempt to impress the opposite sex fails. Female readers, in contrast, are likely to interpret the tale as a classic case of testosterone poisoning, of a male's physiology getting the best of him, diverting all his attention to strutting. Of course we can't be sure, but to me, A74 looked distinctly embarrassed. Certainly, his rapid glances after the fall suggested his concerns for whether he'd had an audience for his mishap. His rapid move away from the ditch and into a macho stance looked like an attempt to recoup from a clumsy move.

For us to positively assert that A74 felt embarrassed, however, we'd have to know more about several other kinds of cognitive abilities. To be embarrassed, A74 would require a sense of self and of what others think about him. He would have to be able to imagine that others might ridicule him or think less of him because he's a klutz. He would have to imagine that F38 might leave him because he looks silly, awkward, and nothing like the stud she thought she was consorting with.

Although we can't answer these questions, there's no greater source of entertainment than to imagine what animals might feel, or to imagine that they're as silly, cool, and aware as the cows in Gary Larson's cartoons.

Mark Twain noted that human beings are the only species that blushes, or needs to. Maybe. Maybe not.

GORDON M. BURGHARDT | *University of Tennessee*

Temperature and Temperament

Snakes may not seem the most personable or emotive of animals, but that may be because we approach them with our own emotions on our sleeve and our critical reason tucked far behind. To be sure, snakes lack the mobile facial muscles of mammals or the rich vocal repertoire of birds and mammals: Monkeys scream, birds twitter, snakes do neither. Nonetheless, snakes do have ways of conveying their emotional states to us. Many humans know this; we're just reluctant to concede snakes any ability to subjectively experience or process emotions in ways comparable to "higher animals."

Snakes respond to threatening or dangerous situations in different ways. When a bull snake hisses and strikes or a rattlesnake coils and rattles, we're seeing behavior akin to irritation or anger. When a snake flees quickly or writhes violently and emits foul-smelling secretions when picked up, we're seeing behavior comparable to fear. Some species, such as habu (a highly venomous pit viper from Okinawa), are so irritable that one snake lightly touching another with a tongue flick can trigger an intense, jerky avoidance reaction from the animal so touched. Anacondas are very prone to strike when handled, which is why they make

Garter snakes often secrete a foul-smelling fluid from their cloacal (anal) glands if they are handled, a clear sign of discomfort and fear.

much poorer pets than other large snakes, such as boa constrictors or some pythons.

Along with emotions, snakes have personalities, and their personality differences are observable within a species and even among individuals. We've studied the antipredator behavior of garter, ribbon, water, and related snakes for many years. Often we begin by observing newly born or hatched snakes. Not only do different species, even closely related ones, differ in their defensive personalities, but also such differences run in families. Some litters are much more prone to show body flattening, puffing up, striking, or fleeing than others. However, even in a species that's typically very feisty when approached or touched, some individuals are very placid and "tame." Furthermore, the ability to alter personality—to turn an aggressive snake into a peaceable one, for instance—varies by individual. Some respond more to friendly treatment than others do.

People familiar with snakes quickly learn that with serpents—as with dogs, cats, or humans—there are times when it's a bad idea to invade an animal's space. With snakes, whether they've fed recently affects their temperament, as does their body temperature. Since snakes are ectothermic, or cold-blooded, their temperature can influence whether they flee, flatten, puff up, rattle, hiss, or strike when approached. Even how they've been handled weeks before can bear

on what emotions they display. So can drugs. Valium and Prozac alter ophidian emotional responses in much the same way that they change the moods of dogs and people.

All these observations suggest that snakes are more than robots performing mechanical behavior. However, definitive evidence for their emotionality is likely to come only when we are able to test whether snakes have brain processes underlying their emotions comparable to those of mammals.

Anyone who's kept, bred, or raised snakes is most aware of their different temperaments and takes these into account in selecting animals to keep or release, breed or trade, buy or sell, or even assign for care. Most zookeepers, while using anthropomorphic terms to describe the snakes' temperaments, insist they're not implying that the snakes actually experience different emotions. But I think there's a good chance that they do exactly that. If so, how we keep and treat snakes in captivity may need considerable rethinking.

DEBORAH FOUTS AND ROGER FOUTS | *The Great Ape Project and the Chimpanzee and Human Communication Institute, Central Washington University*

Our Emotional Kin

Our emotions are one of our most important adaptations for survival—not just for humans but for most, if not all, mammals. It's through our emotions that we detect and flee from danger, that we experience the joys of attachment and the sorrow of loss. Without emotions a mother would never care for her children nor they for her, and our family ties would become useless, frayed ends attached to nothing.

Why is it that for so long we've assumed that other animals don't share these essential emotions? It's because in our arrogance-induced ignorance we've chosen to look the other way when our fellow animals suffered. We've also used a rubber yardstick to measure our compassion as real and intentional but theirs as a thoughtless reflex.

In our more than thirty years of living with and studying chimpanzees, we've come to believe that we share all our emotions with them. Such differences that exist are merely of degree—differences that probably have a greater range within our own species than between ours and theirs. Of the thousands of emotional experiences that we've observed and shared with chimpanzees over the years, we'd like to share a few with you.

Chimpanzee Washoe lovingly grooms her son Loulis. These peaceful moments of bonding are enjoyed by both.

Compassion for Fellow Chimpanzees

Moja and Dar, chimpanzees who are social siblings, have been a part of Washoe's family for many years. Moja, the oldest sister, was known to bully and tease her younger brother, Dar, when he was young. It took a number of years for Dar to fully trust her and to allow their friendship to flourish. One cool fall day, Dar and Moja sat side by side and Dar began touching a sore on his arm. Moja looked over at Dar, then looked at his sore and kissed him on the ear. Dar again touched his sore, and Moja leaned over and kissed it and they began to groom. Sometimes a kiss will make it better.

Grief, Sadness, and Depression

Washoe's infant son, Sequoyah, died after losing a valiant battle with severe pneumonia. Our family, human and chimpanzee, grieved. Because Washoe's pediatrician needed to have access to Sequoyah, he had been separated from her when he died. The task of breaking the sad news to her fell to Roger.

Early morning on the day following the baby's death, Roger went in to see Washoe. As she saw him walk in she began to sign BABY, cradling her arms, raising her eyebrows to emphasize the question. Roger leaned toward her and signed BABY DEAD BABY GONE BABY FINISHED. Washoe watched and dropped her cradling arms from the sign BABY to her lap. She moved slowly to a far corner and looked away, her eyes vacant. For the next three days, Washoe would ask Roger BABY? And Roger would reply BABY DEAD. Washoe sat in the corner, refusing to interact with anyone, human or chimpanzee. Finally she began refusing meals. Her anguish deepened with each passing day, and she became more depressed. It seemed to us that because she finally stopped asking and withdrew, she'd come to understand the finality of Sequoyah's death. She, like many humans, was unable to accept death easily. Her daily question about her baby was very much like human denial. It was as if she were asking, "Are you absolutely sure he is dead?"

It was only after two more weeks, when Washoe adopted baby Loulis, that she finally pulled out of her life-threatening depression.

Homecoming

It took thirteen long years to secure funding and to build a spacious new home for Washoe and her chimpanzee family. Finally, the Chimpanzee and Human Communication Institute was complete, and the time for the move was upon us. Washoe, Moja, Tatu, Loulis, and Dar woke up in their new home. As Washoe stared out the window onto her sunlit garden, she began to scream with a delight usually saved for Christmas morning. She hugged Loulis and ran toward the glass doors and signed OUT, OUT. Our plan had been to give the chimpanzees two

weeks to acclimate to their new home, but they spent those first days begging to go OUT. So on the third day, after breakfast, we told them, TODAY YOU GO OUT. Washoe leaped up and parked herself by the hydraulic door that leads to the outside upper deck. She waited there for more than an hour, with Loulis right behind her. He seemed a little nervous and needed his mother's reassurance.

Finally, the door slid up. Loulis swaggered, then seemed to think better of it and sat back down. Washoe waited for him patiently, but Dar squeezed by and exploded out the door and down the stairs to the ground. He raced across the grass field with an ecstatic movement that looked like quadrupedal skipping. He headed directly for the far terrace, climbed to the top of the thirty-two-foot-high fence, and gazed out over Ellensburg. Then he turned toward us and let out a loud pant-hoot of happiness. Washoe was the next one out. She stood upright and surveyed the terraces, the garden, and the familiar human faces at the observation window below. Stretching out her leg, she touched her toes to the first step and then pulled them back. Then she noticed Debbi was standing near the fence. Washoe walked over with a spring in her step, reached through the fence, and kissed Debbi through the wire. This was clearly her way of saying "thank you," and Debbi was moved to tears by Washoe's thoughtful gratitude.

Now Loulis edged out the doorway. Washoe climbed down a few steps to encourage him, then looked back and signed HUG to him. Loulis was clinging to the fence. Tired of

A pensive Moja models her favorite sweatshirt. As some human older siblings do, she bullied and teased her younger brother Dar.

waiting, Washoe climbed the rest of the steps to the ground. Standing upright, she stamped her feet and thumped the back of her hand against the observation window, reminding the observing visitors of her territory. Then she put her lips to the glass and delivered kisses to a few of her friends, including Dr. Fred Newschwander, her veterinarian.

Words of Comfort

While acting as a parent volunteer on a high school ski trip one Saturday, Roger fell and broke his arm. The following Monday, he came into the chimpanzee area with his broken arm in a sling, but not in a cast, to contain it until the bones knitted.

The chimpanzees must have seen the pain he was trying to hide, because instead of giving their usual, raucous, pant-hoot morning greeting, they all sat very still and intently watched him. Washoe signed HURT THERE, COME, and Roger approached and knelt down by the group. Washoe gently put her fingers through the wire separating them, and Roger moved closer. She touched him, then kissed his arm. Tatu also signed HURT and touched him.

What is perhaps most amazing about their reaction was that ten-year-old Loulis didn't ask Roger for his usual CHASE game, forbearing to ask for this favorite form of play, in fact, until several weeks later, when Roger's arm was on the mend.

AUTHORS

Marc Bekoff, a former Guggenheim Fellow, is professor of organismic biology at the University of Colorado, Boulder, and a Fellow of the Animal Behavior Society. He is the author or editor of twelve books, including *Species of Mind: The Philosophy and Biology of Cognitive Ethology* (with Colin Allen, MIT Press, 1997); *Animal Play: Evolutionary, Comparative, and Ecological Approaches* (edited with John Byers, Cambridge University Press, 1998); *Encyclopedia of Animal Rights and Animal Welfare* (Greenwood Publishing Group, 1998); and *Nature's Life Lessons: Everyday Truths from Nature* (with Jim Carrier, Fulcrum, 1996). Bekoff's work has been featured on *48 Hours,* National Public Radio, the Discovery Channel, and National Geographic Television, and in *Time, Life, U. S. News & World Report,* and the *New York Times.*

Colin Allen is an associate professor of philosophy at Texas A&M University. He is coauthor (with M. Bekoff) of *Species of Mind* (MIT Press, 1997); coeditor (with M. Bekoff and G. Lauder) of *Nature's Purposes* (MIT Press, 1998); and coeditor (with D. Cummins) of *The Evolution of Mind* (Oxford University Press, 1998).

Roland C. Anderson is the Puget Sound biologist at the Seattle Aquarium, where he has worked for twenty-two years. He has a particular interest in the behavior of cephalopods, especially in the play, personality, and emotions of octopuses. His current goal is to raise and display a giant Pacific octopus ("The Shadow") weighing more than a hundred pounds.

Luděk Bartoš is founder and head of the Ethology Group at the Research Institute of Animal Production in Prague, Czech Republic. He specializes in the ethology and physiology of animal behavior, particularly among deer.

Benjamin B. Beck is associate director for biological programs at the National Zoological Park, Smithsonian Institution, Washington, D.C., and adjunct professor of biology at George Mason University in Fairfax, Virginia. He currently studies cognitive aspects of adaptation by captive-born primates when they are reintroduced to the wild.

Anne Bekoff is professor of environmental, population, and organismic biology at the University of Colorado, Boulder, specializing in embryology and neurobiology. Among her many published works are articles on development of fetal behavior and hatching in chicks.

Joel Berger is a professor at the University of Nevada in Reno and a research associate with the Wildlife Conservation Society in New York. His work focuses on behavioral ecology and conservation biology of mammals. Berger, who received his Ph.D. at the University of Colorado, has written books on black rhinos, bison, and wild horses.

Ruud van den Bos is assistant professor at Utrecht University's Animal Welfare Centre in Utrecht, Netherlands. His current research interests are theory of mind in human and nonhuman primates, and the evolution of neuronal networks underlying emotional and cognitive control of behavior as it concerns animal welfare, especially in cats.

Sarah (Sally) T. Boysen is professor of psychology at Ohio State University and director of the Comparative Cognition Project at the Ohio State University Chimpanzee Center. In addition to numerous scientific publications on comparative cognition, Dr. Boysen's research has been featured on national and international television.

Gordon M. Burghardt is an Alumni Distinguished Service professor in the departments of psychology and ecology and evolutionary biology at the University of Tennessee, Knoxville. He studies the genetic, developmental, and experiential aspects of reptile behavior using various methods, including molecular genetics, behavioral observation, experiments, brain imaging, and critical anthropomorphism. His current interests lie in the plasticity of neonatal snake behavior and turtle and lizard play.

Richard W. Byrne is professor of evolutionary psychology at the University of St Andrews, Scotland, founder-member of the Scottish Primate Research Group, and vice president of the International Primatological Society. His book *The Thinking Ape: the Evolutionary Origins of Intelligence* (Oxford University Press, 1995) was honored with the British Psychology Society's Book Award in 1997.

Michel Cabanac, M.D., is professor of physiology at Laval University Faculty of Medicine in Quebec. From the study of temperature regulation, he became interested in the role of pleasure as a motivation for behavior and in behavioral fever in species from flatworms to humans. His work now examines emotional fever and animal emotion.

Anne Innis Dagg, who has taught for many years at the University of Waterloo, Ontario, has studied giraffes and camels in Africa and written books in part about their behavior. Her current focus is working to reduce the number of mice and rats injured and killed for research projects that produce no useful results.

Frans B. M. de Waal is C. H. Candler professor in the psychology department of Emory University, and director of the Living Links Center for Ape and Human Evolution at the Yerkes Regional Primate Research Center in Atlanta. His latest books include *Good Natured* (Harvard University Press, 1996) and *Bonobo: The Forgotten Ape* (University of California Press, 1997).

Christine Drea is assistant professor of biological anthropology and anatomy at Duke University, where she currently studies lemurs. She received her Ph.D. in psychobiology at Emory University and postdoctoral training at the University of California, Berkeley. Her interests span social cognition, behavioral and morphological development, and reproductive endocrinology. She has a special fondness for hyenas.

Francine L. Dolins received her Ph.D. in cognitive psychology and behavioral primatology from the University of Stirling (UK). A former employee of the Humane Society of the United States, she is an assistant professor of psychology at Polytechnic University in New York. Her most recent publication is *Attitudes to Animals: Views in Animal Welfare* (Cambridge University Press, 1999). Her interests are in animal spatial cognition, navigation, foraging behavior, and animal welfare. **Christopher G. Klimowicz**, a stained-glass artist and children's book author and illustrator, obtained his B.F.A. from Seton Hall University and Carnegie Mellon University

Lee Alan Dugatkin is associate professor of biology at the University of Louisville in Kentucky. His research interests include cooperation, altruism, mate choice, and the interaction of cultural and genetic evolution. He is the author of *Cooperation among Animals* (Oxford University Press, 1997) and *Cheating Monkeys and Citizen Bees* (The Free Press, 1999).

John C. Fentress is adjunct professor in psychology, Dalhousie University, Nova Scotia, and the University of Oregon. He received his Ph.D. in animal behavior at Cambridge University in 1965, during which time he lived with the wolf, Lupey. His interests include animal behavior, development, and neuroscience.

Roger and Deborah Fouts are codirectors of the Chimpanzee and Human Communication Institute at Central Washington University in Ellensburg, Washington. In addition, Roger Fouts serves the university as Distinguished Research Professor of psychology. In 1981 they founded Friends of Washoe, a nonprofit organization dedicated to the welfare of chimpanzees. The Foutses, who also serve on the advisory board for the Great Ape Project, work to improve the treatment of chimpanzees in captivity by promoting humane care programs. Together the Foutses have published more than seventy-five

articles and books, including Roger Fouts's celebrated memoir *Next of Kin: What Chimpanzees Have Taught Me about Who We Are* (William Morrow & Co., 1997), written with Stephen T. Mills.

Michael W. Fox is the author of more than forty books and a nationally syndicated newspaper column, "Ask Your Animal Doctor." He lectures worldwide on animal welfare, behavior, conservation, and bioethics; serves as senior scholar, bioethics, for the Humane Society of the United States; and has a veterinary degree from London's Royal Veterinary College, a Ph.D. in medicine, and a D.Sc. in ethology/animal behavior, both from London University.

Toni Frohoff is research director for TerraMar Research. She specializes in marine mammal behavior and consults internationally for government and nonprofit agencies. She received her Ph.D. in behavioral biology and her M.S. in wildlife and fisheries sciences. Currently, she is editing a book on human-dolphin interactions for Sierra Club Books/Random House.

Jane Goodall is a world-famous ethologist whose landmark work with chimpanzees in Gombe, Tanzania, forever altered the very definition of "humanity." Dr. Goodall founded the Jane Goodall Institute in 1977 to help spread her conservation message. The recipient of numerous honors and awards, Dr. Goodall currently serves as National Geographic Society explorer-in-residence.

Marc Hauser is a professor at Harvard University in the department of psychology and the program in neurosciences. He is a member of the Mind, Brain, and Behavior Program at Harvard; a recipient of the National Science Foundation Young Investigator Award; and author of *The Evolution of Communication* (MIT Press, 1996) and *Wild Minds: What Animals Really Think* (Henry Holt, 2000).

Bernd Heinrich joined the University of Vermont in 1980, where he established a program to investigate the behavioral ecology of ravens. Prior to that Dr. Heinrich was professor of entomology at the University of California, Berkeley. He earned his Ph.D. at UCLA, studying mechanisms of thermoregulation in sphinx moths.

Denise L. Herzing, research faculty of biological sciences at Florida Atlantic University in Boca Raton, serves as research director of the Wild Dolphin Project, for which she has completed fifteen years of a long-term investigation of the Atlantic spotted dolphins inhabiting Bahamian waters. She is well known for her work with the Society for Marine Mammology and the European Cetacean Society, and through numerous publications and television appearances.

AUTHORS

Kay E. Holekamp attended Smith College and received her Ph.D. at the University of California, Berkeley. She is currently professor of zoology at Michigan State University. Her research focuses on why and how animals leave one social group and join another. She has been studying spotted hyenas in Kenya since 1988. **Laura Smale,** associate professor of psychology at Michigan State University, received both her B.A. and her Ph.D. degrees at the University of California, Berkeley. In addition to work on spotted hyenas, she studies rodents to determine how brain structure and function differ between diurnal and nocturnal mammals.

David Macdonald is director of Oxford University's Wildlife Conservation Research Unit and an A. D. Professor at Cornell University. In addition to carrying out his research, he writes books and makes documentary films. In Britain, Dr. Macdonald is the only author to have twice won the Natural History Writer of the Year Award, and in a BBC poll his film *Meerkats United* was voted best nature film ever.

Carron A. Meaney is a research associate at the Denver Museum of Natural History, curator adjoint at the University of Colorado Museum, and an environmental consultant. She studies mammals and is presently investigating recreational impacts on small mammals and the natural history of a threatened subspecies of meadow jumping mouse.

Douglas Mock is professor of zoology at the University of Oklahoma, where his primary areas of study include siblicide in egrets, the dynamics between dual-parenting house sparrows, and the role of male hormones in avian brood-rearing versus philandering. He is co-author, with Geoffrey A. Parker, of *The Evolution of Sibling Rivalry* (Oxford University Press, 1997).

Cynthia Moss has spent the past thirty-two years in Africa studying elephants and working for their conservation. In 1972 she started the Amboseli Elephant Research Project in Kenya, which she continues to direct while working for the African Wildlife Foundation. The author of five books, including *Elephant Memories* (University of Chicago Press, 2000) and *Echo of the Elephants* (W. Morrow, 1992), she has also made several award-winning documentaries.

Ruth C. Newberry is assistant professor in the department of animal sciences and the department of veterinary and comparative anatomy, pharmacology, and physiology at Washington State University. A member of the university's Center for the Study of Animal Well-being, she studies the behavior of chickens and pigs with a view to improving their welfare.

Jaak Panksepp is distinguished research professor emeritus, at Bowling Green State University. His current work investigates how the social bonding and play mechanisms of the brain relate to childhood disorders such as autism and ADHD. He is the author of *Affective Neuroscience: The Foundations of Human and Animal Emotions* (Oxford University Press, 1988).

Irene Pepperberg received her S.B. from MIT and graduate degrees from Harvard. She is an associate professor at the University of Arizona and a visiting associate professor at the MIT Media Lab. A former Guggenheim Fellow, she is also a Fellow of the Animal Behavior Society, the American Psychological Association, the American Psychological Society, and the American Ornithologists' Union.

Frans X. Plooij, director of the International Research Institute on Infant Studies, the Netherlands, studied chimpanzees in Gombe from 1971-73, and at the University of Cambridge. He obtained his Ph.D. at the University of Groningen, the Netherlands, where he then served as a professor in the department of developmental and experimental clinical psychology. He is the co-author of *Why They Cry* (Thorsons/HarperCollins, 1996), which was published in seven languages.

Joyce Poole, author of *Coming of Age with Elephants: A Memoir* (Hyperion, 1996), has been studying the behavior of African elephants and working for their conservation since 1976. She has pioneered research on vocal communication and on the sexual and aggressive state of musth in males. She lives in Kenya, where currently she is attempting to describe the vocal repertoire of the Amboseli elephants.

Anne Rasa studied at the Universities of London and Hawaii and at the Max Planck Institute in Seewiesen, Germany. She has held various positions at German universities while investigating dwarf mongooses, and for five years spent half of the year living in the bush in Kenya. Formerly professor of ethology at the University of Pretoria, she now holds the position at Bonn University, Germany. She has published more than sixty scientific papers, and the book *Mongoose Watch (Die perfekte Familie)* (Doubleday Press, 1986). Her research findings have been made into five films for television.

Naomi A. Rose is the marine mammal scientist with The Humane Society of the United States. She received her Ph.D. from the University of California, Santa Cruz, where she studied the behavior of killer whales, elephant seals, and other marine mammal species. She has appeared on various television news programs, testified at federal and state legislative hearings, participated in national and international conservation meetings, and published articles and reviews in animal protection and conservation publications.

Clinton R. Sanders is professor of sociology at the University of Connecticut. He is associate editor of the *Journal of Contemporary Ethnography* and coeditor of Temple University Press's *Animals, Culture, and Society* series. His most recent book is *Understanding Dogs: Living and Working with Canine Companions* (Temple University Press, 1999).

Sue Savage-Rumbaugh is professor of biology and psychology at the Language Research Center at Georgia State University. She has been studying ape language for more than two decades. She and Roger Lewin wrote of her pioneering work in *Kanzi: The Ape at the Brink of the Human Mind* (John Wiley & Sons, 1996).

Ronald J. Schusterman is a research marine biologist at the University of California, Santa Cruz, and professor emeritus of biology and psychology at California State University, Hayward. His current research emphasis is on evaluating the impacts of anthropogenic noise on seals and sea lions.

Alexander Skutch is the author of numerous professional articles and books on birds, including *Parent Birds and Their Young* (University of Texas Press, 1976) and *The Minds of Birds* (Texas A&M University Press, 1996). The winner of many professional awards, he has studied a wide variety of birds in their native habitats for more than seventy years. Now in his late nineties and living in Costa Rica, he is still actively studying and writing about birds. Few others have made such long-term and substantial contributions to the field of ornithology.

Barbara Smuts received a Ph.D. in behavioral biology from Stanford University and is currently professor of psychology at the University of Michigan. She has studied wild chimpanzees, savanna baboons, and bottlenose dolphins, and has published many scientific articles and two books, including *Primate Societies* (coeditor, University of Chicago Press, 1987) and *Sex and Friendship in Baboons* (Harvard University Press, 1999).

Marek Špinka works as a senior researcher at the Research Institute of Animal Production in Prague, Czech Republic. His main research interest is farm animal behavior, especially maternal and social behavior in pigs and cattle.

Elizabeth Marshall Thomas often writes on the subject of animals. Her books include *The Hidden Life of Dogs* (Houghton Mifflin, 1993); *The Tribe of Tiger: Cats and Their Culture* (Simon & Schuster, 1994); and most recently, *The Social Lives of Dogs: The Grace of Canine Company* (Simon & Schuster, 2000). She lives in New Hampshire in a large household that includes four parrots, five dogs, and six cats.

Michael Tobias has written or edited twenty-five books, including *Kinship with the Animals* (Beyond Words, 1998), and *World War III: Population and the Biosphere at the End of the Millennium* (Continuum International, 1998). As a film director and producer, Tobias has more than 150 to his credit, including the award-winning series *Voice of the Planet* and *Kids and Animals: A Healthy Partnership*.

Françoise Wemelsfelder is a research scientist in animal behavior and welfare at the Scottish Agricultural College in Edinburgh. Her interests include animal consciousness, philosophy of science, and in particular, the ability of animals to express their emotions through behavior. At present she is working with pigs to develop a methodology for the description of expressive emotional states in animals.

Andrew Whiten is professor of evolutionary and developmental psychology at the University of St. Andrews, Scotland. His principal research interests are the evolution and development of mind in human and nonhuman primates. With Richard Byrne he is the editor of *Machiavellian Intelligence* (Oxford University Press, 1988) and *Machiavellian Intelligence II* (Cambridge University Press, 1997).

Richard W. Wrangham is a professor of anthropology at Harvard University. Since 1987, he has codirected the Kibale Chimpanzee Project with G. Isabiriye-Basuta, promoting research and conservation of chimpanzees in Uganda's Kibale National Park. His interest in the relationship between human and chimpanzee behavior is described in *Demonic Males* (with Dale Peterson, Houghton Mifflin, 1996).

Bernd Würsig received his Ph.D. from the State University of New York at Stony Brook in behavior and neurobiology. He teaches and conducts research on marine mammal behavioral ecology at Texas A&M University at Galveston, where he is also director of the Marine Mammal Research Program. A prolific writer of scientific and popular works, he is currently involved in marine mammal studies in Russia, Hawaii, New Zealand, and the Gulf of Mexico.

SUGGESTED READINGS

Colin Allen and Marc Bekoff, 1997. *Species of Mind: The Philosophy and Biology of Cognitive Ethology.* Cambridge: MIT Press.

John Archer, 1999. *The Nature of Grief: The Evolution and Psychology of Reactions to Loss.* New York: Routledge.

Marc Bekoff, 1998. Cognitive Ethology: The Comparative Study of Animal Minds. In *Blackwell Companion to Cognitive Science.* Edited by W. Bechtel and G. Graham, Oxford, England: Blackwell Publishers. 371-379.

Marc Bekoff (editor), 1998. *Encyclopedia of Animal Rights and Animal Welfare.* Westport, Connecticut: Greenwood Publishing Group, Inc.

Marc Bekoff, 2000. Animal Emotions: Exploring Passionate Natures. *BioScience.*

Marc Bekoff and Colin Allen, 1997. Cognitive Ethology: Slayers, Skeptics, and Proponents. *Anthropomorphism, Anecdote, and Animals: The Emperor's New Clothes?* Edited by R. W. Mitchell, N. Thompson, and L. Miles, Albany, New York: SUNY Press. 313-334

Marc Bekoff, Colin Allen, and Gordon Burghardt (editors), 2001. *The Cognitive Animal.* Cambridge: MIT Press.

Marc Bekoff and John Byers (editors), 1998. *Animal Play: Evolutionary, Comparative, and Ecological Approaches.* New York: Cambridge University Press.

Michel Cabanac, 1999. Emotion and Phylogeny. *Journal of Consciousness Studies* 6:176-190.

Eileen Crist, 1999. *Images of Animals: Anthropomorphism and Animal Mind.* Philadelphia: Temple University Press.

Charles Darwin, 1859. *On the Origin of Species By Means of Natural Selection.* London: Murray.

Charles Darwin, 1871/1936. *The Descent of Man and Selection in Relation to Sex.* New York: Random House.

Charles Darwin, 1872/1998. *The Expression of the Emotions in Man and Animals,* Third edition, with an Introduction, Afterword, and Commentaries by Paul Ekman. New York: Oxford University Press

Antonio Demasio, 1994. *Descartes' Error: Emotion, Reason, and the Human Brain.* New York: Avon.

Antonio Demasio,1999. *The Feeling of What Happens: Body and Emotion in the Making Of Consciousness.* New York: Harcourt Brace.

Antonio Demasio, 1999. How the Brain Creates the Mind. *Scientific American* 281:112-117.

Paul Ekman, 1998. *Introduction to C Darwin's The Expression of the Emotions in Man and Animals,* Third edition. New York: Oxford University Press.

Roger Fouts with Stephen Mills, 1997. *Next of Kin: What Chimpanzees Have Taught Me About Who We Are.* New York: Morrow.

Jane Goodall, 1990. *Through a Window.* Boston: Houghton-Mifflin.

Donald R. Griffin, 1992. A*nimal Minds.* Chicago: University of Chicago Press.

Paul Griffiths, 1997. *What Emotions Really Are: The Problem of Psychological Categories.* Chicago: University of Chicago Press.

Bernd Heinrich, 1999. *Mind of the Raven: Investigations and Adventures with Wolf-Birds.* New York: Cliff Street Books

Denise Herzing and Thomas White, 1998. Dolphins and the Question of Personhood. *Etica & Animali.*

Joseph LeDoux, 1996. *The Emotional Brain: The Mysterious Underpinnings of Emotional Life.* New York: Touchstone.

Paul MacLean, 1970. *The Triune Brain in Evolution: Role in Paleocerebral Functions.* New York: Plenum.

Jeffrey Masson and Susan McCarthy, 1995. *When Elephants Weep: The Emotional Lives of Animals.* New York: Delacorte Press.

Jaak Panksepp, 1998. *Affective Neuroscience.* New York: Oxford University Press.

Joyce Poole, 1996. *Coming of Age With Elephants: A Memoir.* New York: Hyperion.

Joyce Poole, 1998. An Exploration of a Commonality Between Ourselves and Elephants. *Etica & Animali.*

Michael Posner and Marcus Raichle, 1994. *Images of Mind.* San Francisco: Freeman.

Maxine Sheets-Johnstone, 1998. Consciousness: A Natural History. *Journal of Consciousness Studies* 5:260-294.

Alexander Skutch, 1996. *The Minds of Birds.* College Station: Texas A&M University Press.

Marek Špinka, Ruth Newberry, and Marc Bekoff, 2001. Mammalian Play: Can Training for the Unexpected be Fun? *Quarterly Review of Biology.*

Frans deWaal, 1996. *Good-Natured: The Origins of Right and Wrong in Humans and Other Animals.* Cambridge: Harvard University Press.

Kenyan Cape buffalo bulls use their horns to spar over mating rights with area females.

INDEX

TEXT CREDITS

On warm days polar bears frequently lie on the ice with their paws in the air. They are such intelligent hunters that they sometimes cover their black snouts with their paws in order to blend in with their white fur and surroundings.

OPPOSITE: *Humpback whales are acrobats, often leaping belly-up out of the water and crashing down. This "breaching" might come from pure excitement, but may also be a way for them to communicate their whereabouts to other whales or to remove dead skin and parasites.*

ABOVE: *A young orangutan plays, but mother is close by. Young orangs stay close to their mothers, relying on their milk for sustenance for up to three years.*

ABOVE: *Although we can't hear them without special equipment, rats emit high-pitched chirps during play and lower-pitched "complaints" when negative events take place.*

OPPOSITE: *Red deer stags roar to warn others away from their harems.*

PAGES 222-223: *Until they feed, dolphins tend to avoid humans. Once they've eaten, their natural curiousity returns, including their interest in a diver with a camera.*

ILLUSTRATION CREDITS

STAFF

Discovery Communications, Inc.

John S. Hendricks *Founder, Chairman, and Chief Executive Officer*
Judith A. McHale *President and Chief Operating Officer*
Judy L. Harris *Senior Vice President and General Manager,*
Consumer & Educational Products

Discovery Channel Publishing

Natalie Chapman *Vice President, Publishing*
Rita Thievon Mullin *Editorial Director*
Michael Hentges *Design Director*
Mary Kalamaras *Senior Editor*
Maria Mihalik Higgins *Editor*
Rick Ludwick *Managing Editor*
Christine Alvarez *Business Development*
Jill Gordon *Marketing Manager*

Additional Contributors: Laura Foreman (editing); Stephen B. Freligh (picture editing); Julia Duncan (copy editing); Barbara Klein (index)

Book and cover design by Bill Marr, Open Books, LLC, Edgewater, Maryland

Discovery Communications, Inc., produces high-quality nonfiction television programming, interactive media, books, films, and consumer products. Discovery Networks, a division of Discovery Communications, Inc., operates and manages the Discovery Channel, TLC, Animal Planet, Travel Channel, and the Discovery Health Channel.

Library of Congress Cataloging-in-Publication Data on file with the Library of Congress.

ISBN 1-56331-925-X

Discovery Communications website address: www.discovery.com
Random House website address: www.randomhouse.com

Printed in the United States on acid-free paper
10 9 8 7 6 5 4 3 2 1
First Edition

Gray wolves howl to find other pack members, to define their territory for other packs, and to get their pack excited for a hunt. Sometimes, they also seem to howl just for the joy of it.

ACKNOWLEDGMENTS

Marc Bekoff thanks his companion, Jethro, for unconditionally sharing his refreshing and unfiltered dog-view of the world. He also thanks Laura Foreman for editing and re-editing the stories that his colleagues graciously provided and for her great sense of humor about it all, and Mary Kalamaras, Rita Mullin, Maria Higgins, Rick Ludwick, and Michael Hentges for helping with organizational and practical matters too numerous to list. Conversations with Jane Goodall helped shape the book as well. Finally, but certainly not least, he thanks all of his colleagues for taking the time to write their stories about animal emotions, an exercise that for some was not as easy at it might seem. This book is dedicated to all of our animal kin who selflessly share their incredibly diverse and rich worlds with all whose senses are open to their innumerable important stories of what life is like for them—the ups and the downs and the routines of everyday life. This sharing makes our own lives richer and more meaningful. In the absence of other animals this would surely be an impoverished universe.